GLYN SIMON

His Life and Opinions

Glyn Simon—From the portrait by S. Morse Brown, 1966

GLYN SIMON

His Life and Opinions

OWAIN W. JONES

With a Foreword by the Archbishop of Wales

GOMER PRESS
1981

First Impression - May 1981

ISBN 0 85088 694 5

© OWAIN W. JONES

PRINTED BY :

J. D. LEWIS AND SONS, LTD., GOMER PRESS, LLANDYSUL, DYFED

ACKNOWLEDGEMENTS

The author records his sincere thanks for generous grants in aid of publication from :

The Trustees of the Catherine and Lady Grace James Foundation,

The Bishop of Swansea and Brecon, the Right Rev. B.N.Y. Vaughan, and the Trustees of the Archdeacon Bevan Memorial Fund,

The Trustees of the late Sir Michael Venables-Llewellyn Llysdinam Trust,

The Friends of Brecknock Museum.

CONTENTS

FOREWORD

I warmly commend this account of the life and opinions of
Archbishop Glyn Simon. Paying my tribute at his funeral I
expressed the hope that someone would soon write his Life
with all the objectivity and critical care tha the would wish.
After consultation with Mrs. Simon, The Ven. Owain W. Jones
was asked to undertake the assignment. Very many will be
grateful to him for giving us an account which places Glyn's
many-sided work in the context of his times, and especially of
the Church in Wales during the first fifty years of Disestablishment.

The care that Glyn took in preserving his papers has meant
that here are ample materials for a full-scale biography, the
researching and writing of which would take many years. But it
was thought important to have the Life written while memories
of him were still fresh in the minds of those with whom his
wide-ranging ministry had brought him into contact. The
author seems to me to have got the balance right, giving us an
authentic picture of Glyn as he appeared to his contemporaries
and sacrificing neither accuracy of detail nor soundness of
judgement.

This is certainly not the last word. Others will find themselves supplying from memory evidence that qualifies some of
the assessments made here. No doubt those who look back
twenty years hence will see things in a different perspective.
My own belief is that the clarity that comes with distance will
further enhance Glyn's stature.

It was my good fortune to be his colleague on the episcopal
bench for fifteen years at a time when the issues on which the
Church looks to the bishops for guidance were constantly
increasing in number and complexity. Few have done as much
to make real the collective responsibility of the bishops. It was
typical of him that his choice of a subject for his first address

as President of the Governing Body was made after consultation with his colleagues. Despite his frequent lamentations about the volume of papers we are all these days expected to master (not all of which by any means emanate from Geneva) he developed a capacity for patient listening and for the reconciliation of opposing convictions that had not been so obvious at earlier times in his career. This he achieved despite the handicap of failing health that was to deprive us prematurely of his leadership. Reading the Life has helped to keep fresh in me my gratitude for his friendship, my respect for his integrity and my appreciation of his outstanding services to our Church

+ Gwilym Cambrensis

PREFACE

I am grateful to the Archbishop of Wales for suggesting that I should write a Life of the late Archbishop Glyn Simon, and for the Foreword that he has so kindly provided. I am also grateful to Mrs. Camellia Simon for her ready help and for her permission to examine those papers deposited at the National Library of Wales which are not available to the general public.

A larger work was planned. Indeed the Foreword was written for the longer draft. It applies even more forcibly to this shorter version, made necessary by the problems of publishing in the present economic climate.

I owe a deep debt of gratitude to a large number of friends of Dr. Simon for their help and advice. To the names which are recorded in the text and in the notes I must add that of the Rev. Dr. Moelwyn Merchant. In particular I wish to thank the Rev. D. S. Lee for his recollections of the Industrial Chaplaincy at Port Talbot, Canon Edwin Davies for his estimate of his erstwhile Vicar, the Ven. C. Witton-Davies for the letters he placed at my disposal, and the Right Rev. Eryl Thomas for his careful reading and valuable comments on the final draft of the text. But the responsibility for opinions expressed is of course my own.

My thanks are due to the Staff of the National Library of Wales for their help. But, above all, my thanks are due to those Trusts, acknowledged separately, whose generous aid has made possible the publication of the volume.

Newbridge-on-Wye   Owain W. Jones

EARLY YEARS

The life of Glyn Simon, born on 14 April 1903, spans the first seven tumultuous decades of the twentieth century, times of change unparalleled in human history. He was born into a society which had more in common with Anthony Trollope than, for example, with Rose Macaulay (a writer he admired not least because she described with wit and perception the Oxford that he knew and the High Church clergyman with whom he was familiar in the 'baroque' age of Anglo-Catholicism). He grew up in times which were more akin to the age of the stage coach than to the space age in which he died. Even in the Church, usually held to be the last bastion of conservatism, the changes that he saw were remarkable. The churches his father served in Swansea were new ones, built as a result of the confident and restless zeal for church building and church extension of the men of the late nineteenth and early twentieth centuries. The seeds of future weakness were already present though they were hardly noticed at the time. Only in retrospect has it been seen that the Church was failing to keep up with the growth of population ; and it is becoming customary to refer to those years as the period of the decline of the Victorian Church.

The four Welsh dioceses, Bangor, Llandaff, St Asaph and St. Davids, were then, as they had been from Norman times, part of the Province of Canterbury. The campaign for Disestablishment was already in its later stages and by 1920 the Church in Wales became an independent Province in the Anglican Communion, albeit disestablished and disendowed. However, the end of that campaign turned out to be something of an anti-climax, for the world of the Liberation Society, of Nonconformist ascendancy and of Liberal politics was rapidly coming to an end. Even so, the Welsh Nonconformity which he encountered in his youth was militant in its attitude and flushed with the triumph of disestablishment in Wales. He lived to see a different climate of opinion with the coming of the ecumenical age. He called it : "The Age of Documentary Christianity, when a shower of documents, closely typed, differently coloured and very long, descended upon the Church and in particular upon the bishops."

Inside the Church the Anglo-Catholic movement had been highly suspect in the early years of the century but by the 1920s it was riding high. The young Glyn Simon was a zealous adherent though he studiously avoided many of the excesses practised by some of his contemporaries. He had been prepared for this at home, for his father, of whom he was always quietly proud, was a sound churchman of the Tractarian school; but there is no doubt that Oxford influences completed the process. He was to see many changes in that movement. After he retired he commented rather sadly : "Nearly all the ceremonies and so forth that my father and his like-minded contemporaries fought for are now abandoned altogether ; and the old fashioned ' Protestant ' views which they opposed are now the treasures of the ' Catholics '." While in the main he came to terms with those changes, it is significant that towards the end of his life he described himself at a meeting of the Governing Body of the Church in Wales, as "an old-fashioned Anglo-Catholic clergyman".

Born in Swansea, he was named William Glyn Hughes at his baptism on 12 May 1903 at St. Gabriel's parish church. His father was the curate of the parish and had the charge of the daughter church of St. Augustine. Glyn was baptised by David Lewis Prosser, then the curate of the neighbouring parish of Christ Church and later Archbishop of Wales. Prosser seems to have had a puckish sense of humour for he used to refer to young Glyn as ' Mr. Simon's lost baby ', thereby recalling a memorable incident in his early life.

One day when he was just over a year old, his parents, John and Margaret Simon, went to an organ recital as St. Mary's Swansea, leaving him in the charge of his nursemaid, one Emily Louisa Tribe. She was, in the words of the newspaper reports which were soon to appear, "a young woman of about nineteen, nice-looking, well-dressed and of superior manners and conversation". The parents came home to find that Miss Tribe had

13

decamped, taking with her £16 in cash, jewellery to the value of £18 and also young Glyn. She had taken him to Cardiff where she found lodgings for the night. In the morning she left him with her landlady, saying that she wanted to send a telegram from the nearest post office. In fact she took the train to London. The alarm was soon sounded. Glyn was carried off to the local Police Station where a friend of the family claimed him. His parents were notified and they took the first train to Cardiff.

They returned to Swansea in triumph. Over two hundred people gathered on the platform to greet them while hundreds more thronged the approaches to the station. A still greater crowd waited them in Bryn Road where "the neighbours had gaily decorated the Simons' residence with bunting, and amid the blaze and colou rwas conspicuous the motto 'Welcome little lost one'". A few days later Emily Tribe was arrested in London and finally sentenced to two months imprisonment. Glyn's father was so embarrassed by the publicity that he never liked to be reminded of it. For the son it was the beginning of a life which was to provide a good deal of copy for the Press. Indeed a seasoned reporter, the 'Junior Member for Treorchy' of the *Western Mail*, once said of him : "Oh, what a journalist *manqué*."

For some generations the Simon family had lived in Llansawel, in what was then the County of Carmarthenshire. Glyn's grandfather was the first to forsake the family trade of blacksmith for the new opportunities provided by the coming of the railways ; and William Simon was a signalman in Llandeilo when his son, John, was born. Some time later he was Master of the Union Workhouse in that town. Glyn remembered his grandfather as "a charming old gentleman, a churchman and a conservative ; but he was a restless spirit, not at all approved of by my mother, a strong-willed and firm descendant of the Phillippses of Castell Newydd Emlyn". Caroline Margaret Hughes, who was to become Glyn's mother, was brought up in Lampeter where she met her future husband who came to the College there in 1889. John Simon took his degree at St. David's College in 1892 and was among the first students to be admitted to the Theological College of St. Michael and All

Angels, then newly founded at Aberdare. He was ordained in 1893 and was curate of St. Gabriel's, Swansea, when Glyn first saw the light of day. He became Vicar of Brynmawr in 1910 and five years later he moved to Llanfaes. Great changes were in the offing. The Disestablishment and Disendowment of the Church in Wales came into force in 1920 and a new Province came into being. Three years later the new Diocese of Swansea ad Brecon was created. When the new Cathedral Body was formed Glyn met the then Headmaster of Christ College, J. L. Phillips, who said to him : "Tell your father that we have a truly Apostolic Chapter ; twelve of them and all of them ' unlearned and ignorant men '." John Simon was numbered among them in 1931.

Glyn and his sisters, Esther and Nancy, seem to have had a rather sheltered upbringing.

> We had been kept very much to ourselves and knew only very few children of our own age, and certainly nothing of what the average child of our own age was like. In Swansea we had been sent for a short time to a small private school in the neighbourhood. I remember little about it except for a vague idea that I was not very happy there. This impression was repeated when I was sent, while on holiday with my grandmother at Lampeter, to the College School (now defunct) for a few weeks. There was something about me that evidently roused the dislike of my contemporaries, and even in that short time I was aware of unhappiness and a sense of persecution. However, these tentative little attempts to introduce us to school were not repeated, and my parents, when they reached Brynmawr, fell back on governesses.

It is therefore not surprising that when he was sent to Christ College, Brecon, in 1913, the first few weeks "were accompanied by a general sense of bewilderment, misery and acute homesickness". A traumatic experience on his second day at school did not help matters. The Matron gave him permission to write a letter during ' prep '. The Housemaster, Godfrey Lance —known to the boys by the nickname ' Squire '—had other ideas.

> During his perambulations in the room he came and stood behind me. "What are you doing ?", he asked. I replied : "Please sir, I am writing a letter home." Squire decided to have a little fun. "He is writing a letter home", he said to the

15

class at large, to be rewarded by a general giggle such as sycophantic schoolboys can always be relied upon to provide. "Well," said Squire, "you had better tear your letter up and put it in the waste-paper basket ; and then sit on it facing this way until I tell you to go back to your seat. That will teach you not to write letters home in 'prep' time."

Many years later Glyn related this story at an Old Breconian dinner. His audience laughed heartily, rather to the dismay of the speaker for he had not intended it to be funny. As a result of this incident he wrote : "My doubts as to any change of heart in our boarding schools towards such virtues as imagination, sensitiveness and sympathy were re-assessed."

The School House in which Glyn lived until he became a day boy in 1915 when his parents moved to Llanfaes was, in his view, a wilderness "where not even a mouse would have been able to be quiet and safe". The Housemaster, he remarks, took little notice : "Perhaps he thought that this kind of thing was good for the boys, part of that hardening process which public schools are so often advocated for, and which are supposed to breed real powers of leadership."

For the Headmaster, Robert Halley Chambers, he had a great admiration. He gave him "true clasical teaching at its best and I shall be for ever grateful for it". But for him, during his years at school and for a long time afterwards, the chief figure on the staff was A. E. Donaldson. He prepared him for Confirmation.

> On the surface it was all rather like the preparation for the School Certificate, with considerable attention to the Prayer Book and Catechism. He succeeded however in conveying the impression that this was an event in one's life of the greatest importance. The essential moral strength and teaching of the Catechism came out too. He was a sincere Christian whose convictions hone through the reserve which too often hampers us when we deal with the things of the Spirit.

Donaldson also encouraged him to develop what became the distinctive Simon hand.

> I had just begun to make some little progress in Greek. Hitherto I had written in a round schoolboy hand but now began to experiment with a new self-invented writing (I knew nothing of books on script writing and so forth) based on the Greek alphabet.

16

Donaldson told him : "If you avoid eccentricities you may well write a most interesting hand" ; and Glyn was not a little proud of that handwriting when he was in his prime.

Glyn passed through the stages of lower prefect and school prefect and finally became Head of School. In this capacity he had some problems to face because, in the previous year, there had been a "tremendous row", so he wrote.

> A whole group of prefects were degraded and one or two sent down, and a new head prefect was appointed who was widely believed, while still a junior prefect, to have reported to the Head very considerable sexual misdemeanours in which most of the prefects and several leading and popular sporting braves were involved. I inherited the not inconsiderable backwash of all this, making me over-alert and no doubt unduly suspicious of certain goings on, on a much more reduced scale but similar in kind. The actions I felt bound to take did not increase my popularity. It was a relief to me to find that I was able to face this and other disagreeable events.

Meanwhile his foes "contented themselves with some tough stuff on the rugger field".

According to the modern psychologist the earliest years of infancy are the decisive factor in the formation of the individual's attitude to life. The reaction of people to their school-days may be less significant, but it is something of which a person is fully aware. Glyn's reaction to this period of his life is summed up in these words :

> Although I had some happy experiences at Brecon, the price I paid was too high. My confidence in myself disappeared, so far as it existed at that time, being replaced with a considerable shyness, suspicion and distrust of my fellow-men. On the good side I would put the indefinable influence of beautiful archi- tecture and the long history that accompanied it. I was given a classical education by a fine classical scholar, introduced to good English and a sound grounding in grammar and syntax, for which the Latin I learned side by side with it prepared me. On the bad side I was introduced (literally overnight) at the age of ten to an entirely new way of life. In many ways it was brutish and crude ; bullying was rife ; and the average standard of intelligence not very good. But the general bullying and unpopularity which was my lot left me permaanently unsure of myself, shy and awkward with strangers, especially loud-voiced and fluent self-confident people.[1]

Experiences such as these, however, are by no means uncommon and they are often exaggerated in a person's mind. We have no reason to believe that Glyn, like many others, was so unhappy at school that others noticed it. It is certain that his experiences at Christ College left a wound which was slow to heal and it may not have healed completely. He was far too long suspicious and distrustful of his fellow men, especially if they were young students. There was that "considerable shyness" and uncertainty. But there was at the same time a determination and a confidence in his own powers which to some seemed akin to arrogance. Indeed his schooldays may well have developed in him both sides of his character, and may account for some of his apparent contradictions.

At Oxford where he entered Jesus College as a Meyricke Exhibitioner in 1922 Glyn confesses that he enjoyed himself in a modest sort of way. At school it had been necessary to conform. Now the individualist could reassert himself in a society which allowed its members to indulge their tastes, serious or otherwise, with a freedom they had not previously known. One of his contemporaries, Kenneth Thompson, recalls that Glyn's conversation was usually emphatic and tinged with sarcasm : "He had strong opinions and cultivated a sort of Gibbonian style, delighting in giving vent to vigorous and rather heavy phrases, well-rounded retorts or judgements, 'ponderous wallops' as we called them, quoting a rather obscure parody of Gibbon then going the rounds." They had a mutual friend in the person of N. G. Mathews, later Chancellor of Llandaff Cathedral. Glyn sometimes accompanied them when they went to High Mass and Benediction at St. Barnabas and other "high places" of the Oxford scene. But, Thompson remarks, he was never a zealous adherent. He became irritated if things were too Roman, though it was not always clear where the line of demarcation lay.

Frederic Hood was then Librarian of Pusey House. He noted in his diary that he first met Glyn in October 1922 when he came to dine with him at the House.

> Then on 4 December he came again to meet Dr. Green (Bishop of Monmouth at the time). I was then examining chaplain to the latter and in due course Glyn became at Bangor as much of

a disciple and helper of him as I was in the Monmouth days. I have no memory of Glyn being a server at Pusey House though we had a large number of undergraduates in those days. I think Glyn went chiefly to the Cowley Fathers.

He was, Canon Hood continues, "a keen celibate then and devoted to the monastic life". This was a subject on which he was to alter his opinions, but changes of mind never worried him.

Glyn was placed in the second class in ' Greats ' in 1926. He had settled on ordination at quite an early age and he chose St. Stephen's House for his theological college. There he formed a life-long friendship with the present Lord Wicklow whose recollections of Glyn in 1926 are of

> a picturesque young man in bright tweeds with an even brighter green tie ; he was talkative, a good mixer but introspective rather than gregarious. He spent a good deal of time in chapel apart from periods of compulsory attendance. He was a strong Welshman and we used to try to get rises out of him ; as an Irishman the same was my lot.

At St. Stephen's Glyn read for the Honour School of Theology. He and Kenneth Thompson were supervised by the Chaplain of their old College, L. B. Cross, and they were both placed in the first class in 1927. Thus Glyn's record at Oxford was good without being particularly distinguished. He had a quick mind, he read rapidly and widely and he had a retentive memory, but he had no patience for the minutiae of scholarship. The methods of slow and methodical research were alien to his nature. It is doubtful if he could have sat still long enough to pursue that kind of work. Learning, and his was not inconsiderable, was for him a tool that was to be employed in practical ways. He was always consumed with a nervous energy which required a practical outlet. Such an outlet he found in his first curacy.

He was ordained deacon in 1927 at Chester Cathedral and licensed to the parish of St. Paul's, Crewe, where he took charge of a little "tin tabernacle" which was the daughter church. Rebuilt in 1962 it is now the principal church of the parish and Glyn was present at the opening. Lord Wicklow used to visit him on his way to Ireland during the vacations and he recalls : "I always felt grateful that I did not have to work in Crewe, but he worked with a vengeance. On one occasion I was ill and had to see the doctor. He told me privately how greatly he admired Glyn and what a great work he was doing in rather unpromising soil, with no buildings but his little tin church . . . he spent much time in visiting and when I stayed with him I was surprised how many people he knew well. He had painful corns on his feet from the miles he walked on Crewe pavements and cobbles."[2]

It is curious that Glyn should have sought ordination in an English diocese, because in later years he could be quite short with those Welsh clergymen who "crossed Offa's Dyke", as he used to say. But at that time, loyalty to the Province of Wales was not the "shibboleth" that it was to become. Certainly Glyn had a great admiration for the then Bishop of Chester, Henry Luke Paget, as a man of prayer, self discipline, and a great teacher who could speak simply and tellingly on matters of faith and doctrine. Paget was Glyn's model. He trod faithfully in his footsteps and developed the same qualities. Nor did he seek a prestigious parish, but rather a run-of-the-mill industrial area, perhaps in the best Anglo-Catholic tradition of the time. However it has been recalled that his father, John Simon, was heard to mutter darkly : "Whoever's getting him, they are not getting him here" ; so there may well have been some long-forgotten break-down in relationships in his native diocese.

Glyn had a great affection for Chester Cathedral. On his "days off" he generally took the train from Crewe to Chester to visit the Cathedral and to hear the choir singing Evensong. On one such visit towards the end of 1930 he met the Bishop of Chester at the station. Paget told him that he was going to be appointed to an important post in North Wales, adding that the Archbishop of Wales had told him about it at a chance meeting some time before. Glyn was, in fact, an applicant for the post of Warden of the Church Hostel, Bangor. A few weeks later he was summoned for interview and received the appointment. But it would appear that the Archbishop of Wales, A. G. Edwards, although only one of a large committee, had already decided who the next Warden should be. The Bishop of Bangor, C. A. H. Green, immediately invited Glyn to be one of his examining chaplains and added in his canonical manner : "I wish you to proceed to your M.A. degree forthwith."

When Glyn went to say farewell to Bishop Paget, another Welshman was waiting to be interviewed. This was the future Canon Tom Pugh, head of the Chaplaincy Department of Butlin's Holiday Camps. Through the window they saw Glyn walking down the path, and Paget remarked : "There goes a man with a great future."

2

THE CHURCH HOSTEL

The Church Hostel was then a large house, formerly called Craig Menai, situated in Princes Road in Upper Bangor, conveniently close to the University College of North Wales, and overlooking the straits from which the original name of the house was derived. It had been bought in 1886 by the Clerical Education Association of the diocese of Bangor.

Churchmen in Wales had long been concerned about the training of candidates for Holy Orders, but not until the middle to end of the 19th Century had there been any thought of providing much needed financial help for them. By the middle of the century diocesan societies began to provide some scholarships, but these were few and small. In 1870 representatives of the four Welsh dioceses met in Llanidloes for the first Welsh Church Congress and the whole matter of training for ordination was given a thorough airing. The delegates then proceeded to a resolution calling for the formation of Clerical Education Associations in each diocese.

The first to be formed was in the diocese of Bangor. A meeting was called and the Bangor Clerical Education Association was set up. Contributions were invited and the first examinations for the Association's exhibitions were held. These exhibitions were very small, but they represented a significant step forward ; and as the Association's income increased they were able to do better. In 1884 the University College opened its doors to fifty eight students in the erstwhile Penrhyn Arms Hotel in Bangor and this event inspired both churchmen and nonconformists to think that their theological colleges should be sited near the new institution. The Congregationalists moved their college from Bala to Bangor in 1886 and the North Wales Baptist College moved from Llangollen a few years later. It was hoped that the Church Hostel would develop into a diocesan theological college, but no progress was made in this direction and the house was occupied by a succession of distinguished

Wardens who acted as secretary to the Clerical Education Association of Bangor, and later of St. Asaph, entertained ordinands at the University College to tea and sometimes gave them some tuition in pastoral studies. Gilbert Basil Jones, Warden 1922-31, took the unprecedented step of providing accommodation for eight students, giving over the second floor of the house for this purpose. He also furnished a tiny room in the basement as a chapel. The Vicar of St. James', Bangor, was much enraged at this and wrote a letter of protest to the *North Wales Chronicle*. The Bishop of Bangor, Watkin Williams, replied that such a chapel, while in no way interfering with the activities of the parish clergy, might well provide for the University College the sort of function performed by the chapel of Pusey House in Oxford. The Vicar then, with much sarcasm referred to the dimensions of the tiny chapel. The Bishop, however, was not outdone. He wrote in reply giving the dimensions of the Chapel of the Nativity in Bethlehem.

After the Disestablishment of the Church in Wales, the old voluntary associations were replaced by the diocesan clerical education committees which we know today, and the Church Hostel was run as a joint venture by the committees of the two North Wales dioceses. On his appointment as Warden, Glyn found himself acting as warden of ordinands for Bangor and St. Asaph, chaplain to Anglican students in the University College, and "special lecturer" in the Faculty of Theology. This last title was not as grand as it was high sounding, and behind it lay a complicated history.

When the University College started its life in Bangor, Wales possessed three colleges but no university. The colleges prepared their students for the degrees of the University of London. Their tuition was also restricted by the terms of their charters, each of which prohibited the teaching of Theology. However when the University of Wales came into being in 1893, its charter made provision for a Theology Board to advise the University Court on matters relating to the teaching of Theology. How then was the University to make provision for a subject which was banned by the individual colleges ? It was to resolve this difficulty that the denominational colleges were brought into the schemes. Courses of study would be arranged by the University, but the students would be taught at the colleges supported by the churches. The B.D. degree was instituted in 1896 as a post-graduate course and became, in effect, a course of preparation for ordination for nonconformist ministers, because all the candidates for the degree came from the denominational colleges. In 1922 the Bangor Faculty of Theology was constituted and the staffs of the theological colleges were appointed "special lecturers". Basil Jones became one of these and brought the Hostel into the Faculty. Glyn received a similar appointment 23 June 1931 and he lectured to candidates for the B.D. degree on Christian Doctrine and the Philosophy of Religion. In 1934 he and his fellows became Accredited Teachers in the School of Theology, the old stratagem of appointing "special lecturers" coming to an end with a new scheme.

Accompanied by his sister Esther, who was going to act as housekeeper, Glyn took possession of his new domain during the Easter vacation in 1931. He was soon dissatisfied with it and concluded that the whole place needed to be modernized and put on a more economic basis. The plans drawn up for him by the architect, H. L. North, provided for a wing containing fourteen students' rooms (thus bringing the number of residents to twenty two), and also for a chapel which Glyn was determined should really perform for the University College the function of the chapel of Pusey House, Oxford. A. G. Edwards, as bishop of St. Asaph, favoured the proposals and persuaded his Board of Finance to promise immediate payment of half the cost. Opinion in Bangor was not so easily swayed. The proposals were laid before the Diocesan Conference in 1932 and after a good deal of discussion they were approved.

The alterations were completed before the end of the following year. Archbishop Edwards came to preach at the opening service of the new chapel 7 November 1933. He came in a deeply suspicious mood, under the impression that he had been asked to play second fiddle to Dr. Green who had celebrated the first Eucharist earlier in the day.

It was in a rather sultry atmosphere that the little procession moved to the chapel. Matters were not improved when at the entrance to the chapel the Archbishop stretched out his hand to a student standing by the door for a copy of the form of service. The student shook it warmly. However when we entered the chapel the Archbishop saw that half of it was taken up by the Principal and several professors in full academic robes and there was a sensible lightening of the atmosphere.

A happier procession returned to the Warden's study. A tea-party was held afterwards at the College and the Archbishop was full of smiles for everyone. Next day Glyn received one of his characteristic short notes : "I was touched to tears by the service this afternoon. All was reverently and faultlessly arranged, and the doing of it was yours."

Glyn found that Edwards was consistently kind, "asking me over to the Palace (at St. Asaph) from time to time and making conversation easy with witty and perceptive remarks about the current scene". He had already spent long years on the political stage during the battle over disestablishment and, when that was over, he did all that he could to enable the new Province to stand confidently on its own feet. Yet, Glyn thought, Arch-bishop Edwards never really escaped from his "English Estab-lishment" outlook on the Church in Wales. He resigned in 1934 and he died three years later. Glyn was struck by the smallness of the congregation at the funeral : "He had lived too long ; his contemporaries had preceded him or were too old to come ; already to most people in the Province he was part of its history."

Edwards was succeeded as Archbishop by the Bishop of Bangor, C. A. H. Green. As his Warden of Ordinands for some ten years Glyn worked closely with him ; and he has left some perceptive comments on the second Archbishop. Edwards had been distinctly "Protestant" in his outlook. Green was a high churchman and he brought to the diocese of Bangor, which in those days was rather remote and low church, a picture of the bishop's office (and the way in which it was to be put into practice) which mystified and alarmed his flock.

Driven in a red and silver Rolls Royce with a chauffeur in livery, he descended on remote parishes like some visitor from another world, preceded by a shower of careful directions about vestries and accommodation for the bishop and his chaplains. On the occasion of such visits, they learned, the bells of their churches were to be rung joyfully and their organs to be played cheerfully. If there was only one vestry it was to be cleared for the bishop and his chaplains, and the bishop was to be left alone in it. He was a shy man and arrived and departed in organised grandeur.

Archbishop Green started a tradition of ceremonial which has been well maintained in the Province of Wales. Those who were first introduced to that tradition found it something of a mystery if not a trial.

There were various diocesan functions at which ceremonial was considerable and involved. To the astonishment of their friends, prominent and protestant clergymen in the diocese found themselves, on such occasions, richly attired and given styles and titles which they imperfectly understood. Their sufferings were considerable, though occasionally relieved by *soto voce* but telling flashes of Welsh wit. Of none of these things did their Father in God seem to be aware, as he was wholly occupied in the particular acts and ceremonies of the occasion and expected everybody concerned to be the same.

But Glyn also thought that in many ways Green's standards have been only too well maintained, and in some places slavishly followed. Green towered over his generation in scholarship and learning "and so it is small wonder that his influence has been great, and his authority followed without much imagination or regard for changed and changing circumstances".

Green's Visitations were always very thorough. Indeed it seems that he has been responsible for a revival in the Province of that curious anachronism, the Bishop's Visitation. Canon Law laid down that bishops might hold triennial visitations and that law was sacrosanct for Dr. Green whatever the change of circumsatnces. He once began a Charge to the Dean and Chapter of Bangor Cathedral with the question: "What is the purpose of all this ? Why does the bishop want to ask questions about this and that when he is on the spot ?" But he had no answer to give to his own question except to invoke the authority of Canon Law. The Primary Visitation of Bangor Cathedral left a deep impression on the acute observer who stood among the bishop's chaplains. It began with a service followed by the Charge. Then on the following day

26

The Bishop came to the west door of the Cathedral, fully arrayed in cope and mitre and with a cluster of chaplains of one sort or another. The door was opened to reveal the Dean and all the Chapter waiting to welcome their Father in God. Also present. indeed I think she had been duly cited to appear, was the Cathedral caretaker, a little old lady with a black hat and red shawl. She added a domestic touch to the proceedings by stepping forward and loosening the Bishop's cope which had been caught on a nail. She was then dismayed to find herself greeted in Welsh with some question about her duties. Although she was almost monoglot Welsh, she was baffled by the Bishop's way of speaking it, and looked helplessly at the Archdeacon of Merioneth who happened to be next to her. He kindly translated the query into the kind of Welsh with which she was familiar and then translated her reply to the Bishop. Everything was then investigated. To the dismay of the Cathedral authorities, the Bishop even produced a pair of binoculars and called their attention to missing panes of glass all but invisible. When it came to the font, it was discovered that the stopper was jammed and had been in this condition for a long time. The Vicar General (Ivor Pryce, the Diocesan Registrar) was asked to write formally to the Dean about it, even though that functionary was himself present when this shocking discovery was made . . . At the end of the proceedings I had to tell the Bishop that he had made no enquiries about the Cathedral's greatest treasure, the Pontifical of Bishop Anian. He looked disconcerted for a moment and then said : "Perhaps you can give me a brief report about it and we will see if anything needs to be done."

Glyn had been worried about this book, for it was beginning to show signs of deterioration, and he was always proud of the part he played in having it sent to the National Library of Wales for restoration, whence it was returned in beautiful condition. This incident also led him to reflect that, while Green was very methodical, "he proceeded along regular and routine lines, and anything unexpected or off the normal track might well escape the net of orthodox and well precedented action".

Green was always formal and remote. Some thought it was snobbery. Others, like Glyn, thought that shyness was the reason for his inaccessibility. It is more likely that it followed from the high doctrine of episcopacy which he held and which he elaborated in his book, *The Constitution of the Church in Wales in its Setting*.

> It was this that gave this rather shy man his sureness about himself. He was a Bishop of the Catholic Church, and that triumphed over all else. An amusing incident will illustrate this. As examining chaplain I had to consult him about an ordinand who held somewhat latitudinarian views of the Ministry and supported them with quotations from Dean Inge and Canon Streeter. Green said : "You had better have a word with him ; it will probably work out all right. As for his English authorities, say that Canon Streeter remains in the seclusion of his college, and Dean Inge has not been called to any high office in the Church."

Only towards the end of his time in Bangor, after he had been working with him for nearly ten years, did Green begin to soften and share with Glyn some of his interests and experiences. He was, Glyn concluded,

> an Edwardian, almost a Victorian bishop. Church and society act and react upon one another. Green was almost the last survivor of his and society's conception of a bishop and his office. In its own way it was not a bad one, but the context in which it originated and grew has completely and finally changed.

*　　　*　　　*　　　*

Before Glyn took up his duties just after Easter 1931 Archbishop Edwards asked him if he would prefer to take over in the autumn, at the start of the academic year and with a fresh batch of ordinands. "Why," Glyn asked, "is it an unruly house?" He received the reply, "No, but it is a ruleless one." Glyn set to work immediately and began to impose upon the under-graduates a discipline which approximated as closely as circumstances would allow to what was usual in the theological colleges of those days.

His predecessor, Gilbert Basil Jones, formerly Sub-Warden of St. Michael's College and later Professor of Theology at Bishop's College Lennoxville in Canada, had been at the Hostel since 1922. He was a brilliant lecturer and a compelling preacher but his bent appearance made it obvious to those who saw him that he laboured under the considerable disadvantage of ill-health, so that his presence and influence were not always available in the life of the Hostel. Matins was said daily in the little chapel and the Holy Eucharist was celebrated on Wednesdays and Sundays. Towards the end of his time at Bangor Basil Jones was unable to attend many of these services and so the general atmosphere tended to deteriorate. The students were free to plan their evenings for themselves, provided that they were in by 11 p.m., the time required by the College for the return of all students to their hostels or lodgings.

The new Warden introduced a daily Eucharist which all were required to attend. But the students soon realised that they were not ready for this. Few if any had the kind of background and understanding to take willingly to such an innovation and they reacted strongly. In the event a compromise was worked out. Attendance at the Eucharist was made voluntary ; but it was followed by a period of twenty minutes' silent prayer and all were to be in chapel during this time. The students took some time to adjust themselves to this, but, one of them recalls, after a few weeks the atmosphere improved as the value of this corporate silence came to be appreciated and the discipline of prayer gradually understood. Matins and Evensong were said daily ; and the former freedom in the evenings was curtailed for the students were required to be in chapel for Compline at 10 p.m. There were frequent protests at first over this stricter discipline ; but Glyn blandly informed the objectors that, if they felt that they had embarked on the wrong calling, they had better think again and change course if necessary. At least one took him at his word. When the new chapel was built there was a Sung Eucharit at 11a.m. on Sundays. This service attracted a number of visitors, members of the Senior Common Room and their families, and some of the students' girl friends. Glyn was still an advocate of celibacy and frowned on any emotional attachments on the part of his ordinands. He would speak to them, for example, of "dropping little girls for Lent" ; and, while he came to realize that not all were called to be celibates, he would urge them, as he wrote to one on the eve of his ordination : "Don't get married, and don't buy a motor car—for years." Many of the undergraduates came from Welsh-speaking country parishes. Now they were introduced quite abruptly to a largely English environment where Eucharistic vestments, genuflexions and other niceties of ceremonial figured largely, where the smell of incense might be detected on high days, and where Catholic doctrine, and in particular the importance of the sacrament of Penance, were boldly set forth.

The School of Theology had its annual lectures which distinguished theologians were invited to deliver. The visitors were often given accommodation at the Church Hotel. Sir Edwyn Hoskyns came from Cambridge in the spring term of 1934 and on his return he wrote to Glyn : "You and the Hostel reminded me of Sheffield 1910-14. You manage it better than I ever did and with much more imagination. I therefore wish you God-speed in a very important piece of work."

Among the freshmen who presented themselves at the Hostel in 1932 was R. S. Thomas. His future eminence as a poet of international repute was not apparent at the time ; and he himself admits that he was gauche and without the taste for learning in those days. His first impressions of the Warden were of "a slight, red-cheeked, somewhat knock-kneed cleric, with large glasses and a brittle voice". Later he came to think that the high colour was the result of over-studying. He was given to understand that the Warden was capable of giving some students "a proper dressing down" if it was necessary : "I think we would have preferred that to the facetious and sarcastic notices which he was wont to put up in the common room from time to time." Yet R. S. Thomas developed a genuine appreciation of Glyn's sermons in the Hostel Chapel ; and in later correspondence, right into Glyn's time as Archbishop, he always addressed him as "Warden".

Glyn's influence upon his ordinands, whether they were at Bangor or in other colleges, whether indeed they liked it or not, was considerable ; but naturally those at the Hostel were his chief concern. He made sure that all the undergraduates had some knowledge of Greek before they went off to their theological colleges. In their last years he introduced them to the subject of pastoral studies in preparation for the time when,

he used to say, "you will be vicar of Rhosybol or Llanfairyng-
hornwy", two Anglesey parishes which were singled out for
their resonant names. He sought to regulate every detail even
of the private lives of his ordinands both in the Hostel and
elsewhere. He tried to mould them in their reading and thinking and praying, and would struggle hard to overcome any
resistance ; and as one of those students recalls : "He set a
pattern of discipline and austerity, and made sufficient revelation of himself for them to see going on in him that active
struggle to control the will which the Christian Life (rather
Pelagianly speaking) must be." There was one weakness.
Though he thought himself very shrewd, he was in fact a poor
judge of character. The old wound from his schooldays, which
he had not overcome, made him unduly suspicious of the "loud-
voiced and fluent self-confident" person ; and for that reason
he was too easily taken in by glibness of a "churchy" kind.

Glyn had a somewhat élitist attitude in those days, clearly
regarding himself and those who subscribed to the tenets of
Anglo-Catholicism as of the élite. He was unpopular with
many of the clergy for his outspoken and often sarcastic comments on church life in North Wales. His uncompromising
high-churchmanship made him an object of distrust both to
churchmen and nonconformists, particularly the latter who
saw some of the scions of notable dissenting stock attracted
to the churchmanship which he represented. Yet he became a
focus and a rallying point for young priests in the dioceses of
Bangor and St. Asaph who shared his ideals and were concerned
about growth in the priestly life. He was their confessor, their
guide and mentor, and they turned to him with their problems.
One of these was Eryl S. Thomas who was later to follow
Glyn as Warden of St. Michael's College, Llandaff, as Dean of
Llandaff and finally as Bishop of the diocese. He was then a
curate in Colwyn Bay, about to take charge of a district in the
parish which by repute was decidedly evangelical. Eryl received
this advice :

> You are taking on a tough job at St. Andrew's . . . I should
> give up nothing of your Catholicism, outward acts or anything :
> but be very careful to avoid exaggerated gestures and partic-
> ularly aggravating turns of phrase. Prayers, diligent visiting

31

great patience with whimsy individuals, good sermons, together, cannot be resisted when they are summed up in a priest who consecrates all at the altar. I wish you every blessing and assure you of my prayers.

The rapidity with which Glyn aquired the reputation of being an *enfant terrible* is remarkable and he certainly lived up to this role in which he was cast. He had definite ideas on almost all matters and was never reluctant to express them, as for example in another letter to Eryl Thomas when he wrote : "I share your doubts about Boards of Patronage and their ways. We clergy are too hard and calculating and this-worldly ; and our laity, excellent citizens and able men, are, religiously, probably Arian and certainly Erastian." Yet during this time he was becoming known throughout the Province of Wales as a preacher, confessor, and conductor of retreats and quiet days. Those who heard him were tremendously impressed by his clarity of thought and expression, and by the relevance of his teaching. He had no commanding physical presence and his voice was never strong. He spoke softly (had he adopted the attitude of the anti-hero ?), but of the impact of his words there is no doubt.[3]

The University College of North Wales was then a small and compact community compared with what it is today. It was also more strongly Welsh and Nonconformist than it is now. Glyn's task as chaplain to Anglican students was therefore more clear cut than it was to become ; and of his successors Canon T. J. Morris was the first to be faced with a rapidly expanding University College, accompanied by an equally rapid decline in the number of ordinands resident at the Hostel, bringing a new challenge which Glyn did not have to meet. He had been able to concentrate on matters ecclesiastical, leaving the chaplaincy to run smoothly through the new Church Students' Society and the Hostel Chapel.

In his student days T. J. Morris was largely instrumental in involving the Warden in some weeks of discomfort in the Kentish hop fields. He and a fellow undergraduate wanted to do some practical work during the long vacation, and Glyn suggested that they might help on one of the hop pickers' missions. In 1935 the two young men went to work on the St. Augustine

(Stepney) Mission at Five Oak Green, near Paddock Wood in Kent. For the next three years the mission was staffed for a fortnight by the Warden and his students. "Physically the whole show was pretty rough," Tom Morris recalls, "and the camping arrangements were very crude." It was not really Glyn's line of country, but he put up with it bravely. In the second year he had a bad attack of 'flu and he long remembered "the misery of the train journey back to North Wales which I had to make before I was fully recovered". He was later invited to set down his impression of his hop picking adventures :

We worked mostly on Tapfield's farm. where our camp was, and two or three farms nearby, occasionally making a foray, with a collapsible harmonium which we pushed on a trek cart, to a farm where there had been no mission. The value of the Mission, at least as a civilising influence, we soon grasped after going to camps where there had been none. One's memories are by now confused (it is almost twenty-five years ago) but rich and varied. There is the memory of the daily Mass in the little church at Five Oak Green, and the sense of shock at finding the village to be apparently heathen ; only two or three seemed interested in the Church, a great contrast to what was then to be found in North Wales villages. There were the kind and gentle Father Asher and Father Raven preaching original sermons to the hop-pickers' children who crowded the church on Sunday mornings. There were the hop-pickers, terrified of the dark and crowding the pubs in the evenings, singing and shouting because they were afraid, and the village policeman making rare appearances on a bicycle on which he circled round at some distance because he was afraid of the pickers. There were the fathers and uncles and male admirers who came down on Sundays in charabancs piled high with crates of beer (another strange sight to Welsh boys) of which they drank every drop before going back that night . . . There were numbers of lapsed Roman Catholics summoning one to speak sharply to their erring offspring and brushing aside one's protests that one was not of their Church with the words ; "That's all right, Farver, we're all the same" . . . There were dances (endless Knees up Mother Brown) and the concerts in the Mission hut, with infant prodigies doing tap dances and singing (many, many times) "Pennies from 'eaven" . . . There was Mass on Sunday in the hut open to the camp (has one ever been more conscious of the Presence ?). There was preaching on the village green, of which I was terrified ("much too academic", said Father Farley to me after one address which I thought I had reduced to words of two syllables) and lantern lectures among the huts in the evening, when an audience of Nicodemuses multiplied around me in the dark . . . There were the farmers, much more prosperous than those we were used to, with their curiously detached yet vaguely benevolent attitude to their pickers, whom they looked at and housed much as the Southern planters must have regarded their black slaves. There were the gypsies, a somewhat equivocal group, apt to stir up strikes in which they themselves took no part, and the fierce little man facing fearlessly a mob of angry ladies, and quelling a Mirfield student's well-meant attempts at mediation with the words : "Keep out of this, none of your . . . Christianity here" . . . Now, I am told, it is all over ; machines do all the work. I shall always be glad I knew something of hop-picking as it used to be.[4]

Another work of mercy in which Glyn took a personal interest was nearer at hand. In 1932 the Society of St. Francis opened a home for wayfarers at Llan Ffestiniog. It was supervised by a local committee of which Glyn became a member, and he involved himself as much as possible in the work of reclaiming and resettling the tramps who abounded in those days of massive unemployment. He himself hit the headlines of the national press when he set off in pursuit of two young army deserters who had taken to the road. He negotiated their return over a hedge and a ditch somewhere on the road between Bangor and Aber.

Alan Evans (later vicar of St. Thomas, Swansea) was a graduate reading Theology at the Hostel when he agreed to take part in an experiment. He was admitted to the home, Bryn Llywelyn, in the guise of a tramp and lived there as an inmate, receiving pocket money of one shilling and six pence per week. After a month he was promoted to assistant warden and finally took charge of the house while his superior went off on a much needed holiday.

In 1936 Glyn was offered the parish of St. German's, Cardiff but he declined the offer. Two years later he was an applicant for the post of Principal of St. David's College, Lampeter, but H. K. Archdall was the successful one. The Bishop of St. Asaph, W. T. Havard, wrote to Glyn : "I want to felicitate you on the distinction, which after all it was, to be the choice of Wales though the elected was another ; I know you will not be disappointed having come so near and then to miss the Principalship." Some of his friends have thought that he looked at this College with a somwhat jaundiced eye for many years afterwards. It was probably all for the best because in 1939 the Council of St. Michael's College, Llandaff, invited him to become Warden.

3

ST. MICHAEL'S COLLEGE

Even at the time of the foundation of St. Michael's College in 1892, the college designed to provide theological and pastoral training for the graduate ordinand was still a comparatively new-fangled invention, either regarded with suspicion or considered unnecessary. A number of theological colleges were founded in the early 19th Century, notably St. Bees in Cumberland (1816), the Church Missionary Society's Institution at Islington (1825) and St. David's College, Lampeter (1827). But these catered for those men who were unable to go to one of the universities and their syllabuses were academic rather than practical. "The best preparation for Orders," declared an unknown clergyman whose opinion is typical of his time, "is an academical education, and then a year or two of study and practical training in a country parish, not too large to admit of the incumbent giving personal supervision to the young candidates for Orders, and not too small to supply everything which a parish ought to maintain." The academical education was best obtained, if possible, at the univerities, and the colleges which catered for the non-graduate modelled themselves as closely as possible on them. There was a general objection to the idea of theological colleges as we have come to know them. To require further training from the graduate ordinand was thought to be a slur upon the universities. Besides, many of the new theological colleges had come into being as a result of Tractarian influence and so there was a good deal of antagonism both among the clergy and the laity, many of whom were suspicious of what might become a narrow education in an ecclesiastical seminary. By the end of the 19th Century the number of men who went to a theological college after graduating was still small but it was increasing.

St. Michael's College was no exception to the general rule. Founded by Olivia Emma Talbot, a member of the family which gave its name to the town of Port Talbot, it was from the first a strongly Tractarian foundation. It was modelled upon Cuddesdon, the college where the first Warden, Henry Robert Johnson, received his training. Popularly known as "Y Tad", Johnson was then curate of Aberdare where the college found its first home, and he so moulded his students that they came to be known in the Province as "Johnson's men". The first Sub-Warden was Gilbert Cunnigham Joyce, later Principal of St. David's College and Bishop of Monmouth, and the Council included such prominent Tractarians as C. A. H. Green, Frederic William Edmondes of Fitzhamon Court, Bridgend, and Frederick William Beck, the Vicar of Roath.

The early years passed without any episcopal interference. Richard Lewis, Bishop of Llandaff 1883-1905, assented to the Trust Deed drawn up in 1896 which gave him by virtue of his office "such jurisdiction and visitorial powers over and in relation thereto as are exercisable over and in relation to Colleges in the Universities by the Visitors of such Colleges respectively". Yet by this same Trust Deed the College Council was placed in a strong position :

> the education in the said College shall be conducted by Clergymen and Laymen members of and in communion with the said Church and (in the Judgement of the Council) in accordance with the doctrines, principles, liturgy and formularies aforesaid and the education and discipline and regulations of the College shall be approved of by the Council.

But Lewis was succeeded by the energetic and hard-working vicar of Llantrisant, Joshua Pritchard Hughes, a convinced evangelical who was much concerned about ritualism and drink. Hughes was not a little troubled by some of the Anglo-Catholic parishes in Cardiff, and he was also deeply suspicious of St. Michael's College which seemed to be full of all sorts of undesirable possibilities. The opportunity to try and bring it under his control came in 1907 when the College moved from Abernant Park to the elegant Gothic Revival buildings, designed by John Prichard, which had been prepared for it at Llandaff.

The College Council began to arrange a formal opening which the Archbishop of Canterbury was invited to perform. It seems certain that Joshua Hughes shared his doubts with the Archbishop, for the latter replied that he would be happy to come but that he felt it desirable that the Trust Deed should include a clause giving the diocesan bishop certain powers in the affairs of the College. The Tractarians of the second generation were not so obedient to bishops as their predecessors had been, for experience had taught them to be cautious. The members of the Council were determined to hold on to their powers and they replied that they still wished the final decision, in the event of questions arising from doctrine and ceremonial which might raise doubts about the loyalty of the College to the Prayer Book, to be made by the College Council. The Archbishop, Randall Davidson, then stated that he regarded the question as so important that if the members of the Council would not accede to his wishes, then he must decline their invitation to the opening ceremony. They replied, with great regret, that they were not prepared to change their mind and must accept his Grace's decision. In the event, the opening ceremony was performed by Mrs. Talbot Fletcher, sister to the foundress.

During the war of 1914-18 the college buildings served as a military convalescent home. In 1919 H. R. Johnson felt that he was too old for the task of reopening the College, so he became Vicar of St. Mary's, Cardiff, and he persuaded the College Council to appoint Frederick William Worsley in his place. The Council needed little persuasion. Worsley had come to the College in 1914 as Sub-Warden but he had spent the war years in the Forces. This scholar, author, sportsman, and now distinguished Chaplain to the Forces, seemed to be the obvious choice as Warden, to train the new generation of ex-service ordinands whose wartime ordeal he had shared. Worsley began his work in fine style, but as time passed he seemed to lose interest. His son who has left a remarkably frank account of his brilliant but erratic father's career writes :

> My own feeling—it is nothing more—was that the root cause of his extraordinary behaviour all these years was, precisely, *accidie*. Every time he wound up his clock for a new start, it began from that moment running down and he just could not be bothered to turn the key again. Every effort drained out of him with every passing moment. It was a kind of physical impotence . . . the inability to use his talents in any direction which could deeply satisfy him.[5]

When Worsley was appointed to the Deanery there was the same brilliant start followed by a draining of energy, and it ended with his abrupt departure from Llandaff in 1928.

The next Warden was the scholarly and saintly Edward William Williamson, and for the next thirteen years the life of the College was centred on him and on his Sub-Warden, the learned J. S. McArthur whom Worsley appointed to the College in 1925. Their students were devoted to them and their influence on the young men was considerable. But neither were strict disciplinarians, at least by the standards of the next Warden.

Glyn succeeded E. W. Williamson who had become Bishop of Swansea and Brecon. He arrived at the college just before Easter in 1940. Term was over in Bangor but at St. Michael's the Lent Term went on till the end of Holy Week. On the Wednesday of that week Glyn set down his first impressions.

> This is a queer place in many ways and the young men, though pleasant and friendly, are an odd job lot. The chapel is stuffy and small and the services strange in some ways. I have never heard so many hymns in all my life and never so badly sung. This week the young men, following the tradition of this place, have been coming to Mass daily, but walking out during the "Offertory hymn" specially put on for their benefit. I have interfered in nothing except to have priest's wafers (we have square ones here in sheets) to elevate the Host ; and have the lavabo when I say Mass myself. Also I have not been at the door after Compline to shake hands (but I think there is something to be said for one member of the staff doing that) . . . The library seems to need a good deal of overhauling and everywhere there are Arundel prints, I should imagine almost the largest extant collection.

The recipient of this letter was Carl Witton-Davies, later Dean of St. Davids and Archdeacon of Oxford.

It is clear that in the first place Glyn wanted his own staff. Fortune smiled on him and he was able to accomplish his design. The Chaplain of St. Michael's was about to join the forces so Glyn offered the post to Witton-Davies. There was one small problem. Carl had been appointed to a lecturership at Lampeter but the appointment had been suspended because of the uncertainty of the war situation. Now it seems he would be needed there after all. But Glyn was persuasive : "All my own plans, interests and likes will have a serious setback if I miss you from St. Michael's" ; and finally Carl settled for Llandaff. Glyn then discovered that the Sub-Warden, J. S. McArthur was a candidate for the Church Hostel so he wrote to his new member of staff : "The fact that he is will make it easier for us, for it shows that he is not rooted and grounded in Llandaff as I feared." A few days later he wrote again.

Events move. J. S. M., I heard privately, has been offered the Provostship of some cathedral in Scotland. He was hesitating because of Bangor. So I got in touch by telephone yesterday with both bishops (Llandaff and Bangor) and got them (i) to warn J. S. M. of the unlikelihood of Bangor, (ii) of the likelihood of my wanting my own staff, (iii) to urge him to accept the Scottish offer. I hope he does. Then of course you would become sub-warden on his departure and we could get Eric in by next October. Of course there are the usual "hushes" attached to all this and J. S. M. does not know that I know about the Scottish offer.

Glyn was already showing his dexterity in the gentle art of manipulation. McArthur took the hint and went to Scotland. Carl became sub-warden and the team was completed with the appointment as chaplain of E. M. Roberts, later Bishop of St. Davids. Glyn could now proceed to mould the College into the pattern he desired. He wanted it to be a place for the training of priests, if possible of Anglo-Catholic priests. This could not be accomplished in every case but all the students were made familiar with a standard of churchmanship which tended to be high if not extreme. However, he had not been long in St. Michael's before there were other changes which were not of his making. In January 1941 a German land mine wrecked the college buildings, fortunately during the vacation. Temporary accommodation was found in the Canonry at St. Davids and there the College spent the rest of the war years, staff and students helping on the land in their spare time as their contribution to the war effort.

The end of the war brought with it the welcome prospect of a return to Llandaff though still into temporary quarters in the former bishop's palace, Llys Esgob. This had been

taken over by the army during the war and the Bishop of
Llandaff went to live in the Rectory at St. Nicholas, subse-
quently moving into a house on the Cathedral Green. Carl
Witton-Davies had gone to Jerusalem in 1944 as adviser to the
Bishop in Jerusalem on Hebraica and Judaica. In 1947 he was
appointed to the Canonry of Nazareth in the Collegiate Church
of St. George in Jerusalem. "What a romantic place to be
Canon of," wrote Glyn in one of many letters in which he kept
his former colleague informed about the movements of the
college. "We hope to get to Llandaff in October. It (Llys
Esgob) has been empty since August . . . I do not think that
we can face another winter here" ; and they moved in as
planned by October 1946.

> The maids have performed prodigies in cleaning it down—
> it was in the most horrible condition—and now it is looking
> almost habitable. The chapel is in a very neglected state, and
> as the windows were all blown in, it is almost impossible to
> know what to do there . . . in many ways things are easier
> here than at St. Davids ; the poor quality of much that we had
> there is now plain . . . and there has been a general Te Deum
> at having escaped from St. D.

By the beginning of 1946 the ex-service ordinands had begun
to return. There were sixteen students at the college of which
eleven were newly released from the Forces. "They seem to be
an alien [*sic*] and friendly lot, if not particularly brilliant."
Glyn was at first apprehensive about the possible reactions
of the ex-servicemen, but they turned out to be dutiful and
hard working and by the end of the year he could write :

> The men we have here are, of course, much more mature than
> the juvenile, even infantile types of which we have had too
> many. Running the college is consequently a very much easier
> affair in many respects than it used to be. There are other
> problems, however, and the Government's habit of releasing
> men at odd intervals and without warning is very disconcerting
> and adds enormously to our labours.

In 1945 the college was small enough—there were nineteen
students—for it to be carried off to Cowley, to the Society of
St. John the Evangelist or the "Cowley Fathers", for the Holy

Week retreat, and Glyn wondered how the experiment would work out. It was successful enough to be repeated in 1946 :

> Again at Cowley. What they are making of it all I am as uncertain as ever. They are a nice crowd, mostly ex-servicemen, but what I call religious chameleons, taking their colour from their surroundings, whatever hue they may be. They shy away from the box like anything, and are poor about Lent ; but then so is everybody and what is one to do when bishops smoke like chimneys and attend public dinners in Lent and Passiontide. I feel quite old-fashioned . . .

He had no need to despair. The retreat at Cowley was a very moving experience, and those who shied away from the box were few, such was Glyn's determined and persuasive influence.

Glyn had constantly held up before his students the virtues and advantages of the celibate life. The subject cropped up quite regularly in the discussions in the Common Room before Compline on Saturday evenings, when staff and students were together after their evening meal. When the young men assembled at St. Davids for the autumn term in 1941, they learned, rather to their surprise, that the Warden had married a wife. He had on 7 September married Miss Sheila Roberts of the parish of Rhosllanerchrugog near Wrexham.

Sheila had been a student at the University College of North Wales, and was a contemporary of Carl Witton-Davies. Like him she had been brought up a Baptist and they were both active in the Student Christian Movement of which he was chairman and she was vice-chairman in their final year. Like him she fell away from the family tradition and presented herself to the Warden of the Church Hostel to be prepared for Confirmation. A very able student, possessing great personal charm, Sheila was popular at Bangor and was vice-president of the Students' Representative Council 1934-5. Coming from an unpretentious and thoroughly Welsh home background, she was, one of her contemporaries remarks : "Almost typical of the Welsh student world of her day i.e. a sort of Quaker type spirituality, compassionate socialist politics, pacifist, pro-bottom dog anti-imperialist, emerging into a kind of awareness (with the rest of her generation) of women's lib. and a dawning Freudian freedom." Glyn in his Bangor days was irascibly opposed to all these notions and did not hide his contempt for them. But Sheila was to change all this. Gentle and charming in manner, she was a woman of great strength of will and determination. She kept in touch with Glyn after she left Bangor, seeking his advice and guidance when she began to read for the Lambeth Diploma in Theology. Sometime later she had to give up her teaching post to return home to look after her mother. It was then that the courtship really began. They kept it rather quiet but it did not pass entirely unnoticed. Glyn was frequently away during term, visiting ordinands in university and other centres, and, as Witton-Davies later discovered, returning via Wrexham to call on Sheila. His movements were noticed, and word filtered through to remote St. Davids that Glyn was returning to the shrine of the patron saint via the altar of his lady love. They were married at Esclusham and were well supported by the Staff of St. Michael's College, for Witton-Davies was the best man and Eric Roberts the celebrant of the Nuptial Mass.

The return from St. Davids to Llandaff meant that Glyn and Sheila could now set up house in the Old Registry, the Warden's residence. Their first child died in infancy but in February 1946 Nicholas was born. Glyn wrote to Witton-Davies :

> Nicholas has been christened and behaved very well. The Bishop of Llandaff (John Morgan) officiated. I don't really believe in bishops doing this kind of thing, but as he was using the two front rooms of our house as offices, gratis I may add, and so was practically in on the event, it would have been rude not to ask him. He wore cope and mitre but smeared Nicholas rather than sprinkled him, almost in the manner of Dean Parry with Bridget.

Witton-Davies' daughter, Bridget, had been baptised in St. Davids and the family had provided a bottle of water from the river Jordan for the ceremony. Glyn, however, had reservations about the validity of the baptism because Dean Parry had used so little of the precious fluid.

In February 1948 Glyn wrote again with news of the family, increased some six months before by the arrival of the second son :

Robin is now just six months old and as good a baby as Nicholas was the reverse, which is a very good thing as Sheila's hands are more than full. Nicholas is two on Tuesday ; he is very active and an apparently intelligent child but does'nt bother to learn to talk as he makes himself understood without it.[6]

The family was completed with the arrival of Perpetua, named after the saint and martyr whose day fell close to the time of her birth, but by then Glyn had become Dean of Llandaff.

During the Long Vacation Term in 1948 he was both Dean and Warden, "doing several jobs at once and nearly dead", until he could hand over to his successor at St. Michael's, Eryl Stephen Thomas, then vicar of Risca in Monmouthsire.

It was during the "exile" at St. Davids that Archbishop Prosser once congratulated Glyn on his running of the College because its products, once known in the Province as "Johnson's men" were coming to be recognised as "St. Michael's men". This was Glyn's object and he showed patience and determination in moulding his students into the desired pattern, which represented a sound if monochrome standard of churchmanship. He was hardly a popular Warden. His tongue was still quick and often biting. He still had not shed the elitism of his Bangor days for he once remarked to a Cardiff incumbent, regarding the young men in his charge : "I can put some theology into their heads but I cannot turn them into gentlemen." The college discipline was similar to that in other such institutions at that time. Carl Witton-Davies, for example, found that the routine at St. Michael's reminded him of Cuddesdon where he had been trained ; but Glyn's discipline was probably stricter, more reminiscent of the schoolmaster, and some would say that he was too distrustful or too zealous over petty details. In the present day this kind of discipline would be considered repressive, even unacceptable, and it appears to have been largely abandoned in most if not all theological colleges. In those days, however, the modern reaction against the traditional conceptions of authority and obedience had not made itself felt. Nor had there then appeared the present reaction, which is probably more significant, against the Counter-Reformation spiritual techniques which had been adopted by the Anglo-

44

Catholics of the late 19th Century from Continental sources, and which had been cultivated in the theological colleges of the Tractarian tradition. Not a few devotional manuals of that period have been rendered obsolete because the sensuous—some would say exaggerated and un-Anglican—language, derived from those same sources, has little appeal to the modern mind.

4

THE DEANERY

Llandaff Cathedral has had a long and a chequered history. The pre-Norman church stood near or on the site where in 1120 Bishop Urban started the building which eventually grew into the Cathedral which we know today. After the Reformation it passed through a period of poverty and neglect and by the beginning of the eighteenth century the nave was a roofless ruin. In the 1730s part of the nave was restored under the direction of John Wood of Bath. As the restoration was done in the classical style it has often been described as an Italianate temple set in the ruined Gothic nave but it is best thought of simply as a restoration, if only in part. In the nineteenth century the Cathedral was completely restored, at first under the supervision of Henry Wyatt but after 1847 in the sole charge of John Prichard. Then on 2 January 1941 a land-mine wrecked the nave and made the top of the spire unsafe. By April 1942 some temporary repairs were made in the presbytery and the lady chapel which were used for worship for the next fifteen years.

Glyn's first task, therefore, was to set about the rebuilding of the Cathedral. Some preparatory work had been done but in the post-war world of shortages progress had been slow. It was clear that there would have to be an appeal to supplement the money that would be received from the War Damage Commission and to pay for new work, and a target of £100,000 was set. An appeal committee was formed in 1948 (before Glyn became Dean) and he and Col. Roy Horley were appointed joint secretaries. By the time the appeal was launched Glyn had moved to the Deanery and he took over most of the work relating to it. There were a few minor storms over its administration, for Glyn was often in a hurry and was impatient of red tape (unless that means a desire to have one's own way) but it was eventually carried to a successful conclusion.

The Cathedral Architect, Sir Charles Nicholson, had planned

a fairly conservative restoration. A new feature, or rather a return to the medieval pattern, was the flat hardwood ceiling which he planned, and which required the lowering of the steeply-pointed presbytery arch built by John Prichard. But Nicholson died in 1949 and the Dean and Chapter had to appoint a new architect. Glyn wanted a young man who would be able to look after the Cathedral not only during the restoration but also for a long time after. He consulted the Dean of York, Milner-White, who recommended a young architect from York, George Gaze Pace, who was duly appointed. This was a significant move and one which was to alter the whole course of the restoration. It was also the beginning of a close friendship between Glyn and George Pace.

One task had to have priority. The nave had to be cleared and given a tarpaulin roof so that it could be used for the enthronement of Archbishop John Morgan on 21 September 1949. This gave both dean and architect the opportunity to practise the dogma they were constantly to preach, that a church should be designed as a setting for the Liturgy. The enthronement was one of the earliest occasions, and certainly the first in Wales, when "the sanctuary was arranged after the primitive pattern with the bishop seated above and to the east of the principal altar, supported on either side by his leading clergy, the Chapter of his Cathedral Church, and looking to the west over his faithful people".

Glyn consulted Professor E. C. Ratcliff on the form of service. They removed from the form hitherto used as much extraneous matter as possible, simplifying it and making its purpose plain. At previous enthronements the primatial cross had been held by the archbishop as a kind of crozier. Glyn thought that this was a liturgical error and Ratcliff replied :

> Of course you are correct. The Cross is not a Pastoral Staff. It is true that someone has dug up a picture of a medieval Scottish bishop giving a blessing while grasping his metropolitical cross. But the single solecism of a semi-barbarian cannot be taken to have created a liturgical precedent. The practice was begotten upon an unrestrained imagination by a stained glass window.

The enthronement over—Glyn preferred to think of it as an "installation"—the work of restoration could continue.

George Pace saw his task quite clearly. It was to restore the surviving medieval and nineteenth century work and to wed to them any modern work in such a way that the "cathedral atmosphere" might be recaptured. The building was not large enough to warrant a massive screen, but a division of some sort was required. He therefore proposed to build a reinforced concrete arch and pulpitum to which should be attached a statue of Christ in Majesty ; and Jacob Epstein was the obvious person to execute the sculpture. The arch was first envisaged by Pace as a solid affair. The soffit was to be decorated with a painting of the Last Judgement. Stanley Spencer, one who continued in this century the tradition of the Pre-Raphaelites (who had contributed to the nineteenth century restoration) was the chosen artist. A day-long consultation at the Cathedral with the two artists followed at which the scheme was worked out in detail. When the plans were made known, there was a strong reaction from the public and Glyn received many letters of protest. The prospect of a painting by Stanley Spencer seems to have excited most alarm, but, as it turned out, this was not required. The design of the arch was considerably modified so as to take on a more skeletal form, and there was no place for the painting. Pace found that Spencer understood the architectural problem and did not mind the change of plan.[7]

When the Majestas was completed it was taken to Llandaff where it lay in its unopened crate until it could be placed in its setting. Any temptation to have it photographed before it was placed in position was firmly rejected because it needed to be seen as part of a whole. It was probably the first time that Epstein had to work to a controlled programme, to produce a work that was part and parcel of a building where every part was subordinate to the total impact. When the nave was re-opened in 1957 that impact was quite sensational. What had been accomplished was well expressed by Glyn himself when he was preaching at the King's Lynn Festival in 1964, and his words reveal his enthusiasm for the scheme in which he had involved himself completely :

48

The artist who works for the Church works in a context concerned with the proclamation of certain truths about God and man and their relations to one another, and must obey the discipline which the context imposes upon him. A notable example of this is the great Christus in Llandaff. "Let's go and see the Epstein", people say. But for those who worship regularly there, there is no Epstein, only a great work of art which is part of a whole, harmoniously contributing to the revelation of what a whole building is about. And this has come about through the co-operation from first to last of a great artist with a great architect in the service of a true theological and liturgical understanding of a church and its purpose.

Reactions among the hordes of visitors to Llandaff in 1957 were somewhat mixed. There were not a few who gazed with horror at this contemporary work, forgetting that by this time Epstein was not particularly "modern". Indeed, a member of staff of an art school thought that his students would think that Epstein had produced "a nice bit of commercial for us barbarians in Wales".

There were also designs for the new Welch Regiment Chapel (built and furnished by members of the Regiment at a cost of £22,000), and for a processional way, flanked with vestries, to link the chapel with the Prebendal House. Glyn was an enthusiastic supporter of these projects and George Pace was later to pay a moving and final tribute to him for his help and understanding.

The Dean was a tower of strength in the decisions which had to be taken as to the form of the new work, especially the chapel and processional way, but particularly in the momentous ones on the free standing pulpitum in the midst of the Cathedral . . . Without Glyn Simon's understanding and courage |this unique pulpitum could not have been achieved. In a very real sense it is now his memorial.[8]

All these things were in the planning stage when Glyn was elected Bishop of Swansea and Brecon in November 1953, and he had to leave to his successor in the Deanery, Eryl Thomas, the task of seeing what was planned brought to completion.

The laying of the Foundation Stone of the Welch Regiment Memorial Chapel took place in 1953 before Glyn left Llandaff.

In his address he explained the use to which the chapel would be put :

> First of all, it will be an integral part of the Cathedral ; we shall be able to use it for small gatherings, for special services, for Retreats, which would be lost in the great building itself, or could not have elsewhere in it the seclusion and quiet which this site will offer. But there is more to it than that, and I can hardly express it better than in some words of King Henry V, who, you will remember, himself had a special link with Welsh soldiers, through the Welsh archers whose courage and skill did so much to win him the Battle of Agincourt. In founding the convent of Syon in Isleworth in 1415 he laid it down "that Divine Service shall be celebrated for ever, for our healthful estate while we live and for our soul when we shall have departed this life". This is what will happen here. Every week, on a fixed day, the Lord's Service will be celebrated here, and the Regiment past and present will be held up in prayer before the Throne of Grace . . . And the remembrance will not stop with this life; prayer is not limited by time and space and is not defeated by death. "If we're bumped off, will they sing ' For all the Saints ' for us ?" asked a soldier in the Eighth Army ; "because if they do they're wasting their time". And how right he was. Death in battle or in the army does not turn a sinner into a saint ; and so we continue to pray for all, whether or not they are separated from us by the solemn incident of death. For we believe that not only this world but all the great world unseen is bound about the feet of God by the golden chains of prayer.

These extracts from a brief sermon provide some illustration of the simple and telling homiletic style which Glyn developed and used to good effect in his Llandaff days.

Llandaff Cathedral was also a parish church. In earlier days there had been both a dean and a vicar but now the two offices were held together. Though the demands on the time of the dean-vicar were heavy, Glyn was a diligent parish priest who revitalized the life of a large parish. One who was his curate in those days, Canon Edwin Davies, later vicar of St. John the Baptist, Cardiff, recalls that Glyn knew exactly what he wanted the Cathedral and parish to be :

> It was to be a truly Tractarian church, high church, almost with a Laudian colouring. Yet nothing became his ministry in Llandaff more than the care he took not to hurt or offend the

old-fashioned, almost Victorian, low churchpeople who still lingered there. He won their acquiescence to his policy because they respected what he sought to do and because, like them, he loved the Cathedral and the Church he sought to serve.

The work at Llandaff was based first of all on prayer and sacrament. Every member of his staff was expected to begin the day at the altar, and always there was the diminutive figure of the Dean, wrapped in his old black cloak, bringing all to his Lord in prayer.

After prayer came teaching. Dean Simon, all his life, was a great teacher. I have never heard preaching to excel the sermons that I heard from him in that period. His voice was poor, but he kept to the end of his days a vanity about it that because he spoke clearly he could be heard. As a teacher he was at his best in small informal groups, talking to the youth club about Christian Morals, or speaking about his beloved St. Paul while he sat on a table in front of a spell-bound Mothers Union meeting, casually swinging his left leg whilst the fruits of years of New Testament study poured out in the simplest of language. After teaching came visiting. He set his assistants to visit assiduously but he believed in leading from the front, and as far as his other duties allowed he was on the knocker himself. This he found most difficult because he never had a flow of small talk. But he tried, and ordinary people delighted in his trying. His best visiting was done with the very ill and the dying, and many were comforted in their sorrow by his true priestly concern.

Being the man he was, he could not stand humbug ; and I should fail his memory and my regard for him if I did not state that he like us could be at fault. A brilliant mind and golden eloquence often goes with a quick temper and a biting tongue. So it was with Dean Simon. By the time he came to Llandaff he had learned to control both, but they still overcame his will on occasions. His most infuriating trait, for lesser mortals, was to keep so many details in his head and expecting us to know them by some kind of thought reading ; and although he denied it to the last, several forgotten engagements were saved for the Dean by that most admirable of all Cathedral vergers, the late Robert White.

Always behind the Dean was the constant Sheila Simon. Only those who worked with him can know just how much he depended upon her in every way, not least in judging parish policy and parish people. All Llandaff respected Dean Simon ; all Llandaff loved Sheila Simon.[9]

The move from the Old Registry to the Deanery was a significant one for Glyn, for it had a mellowing effect upon him. He had, in fact, lived too long among students. His experiences at school had made him unduly suspicious of the extrovert character, and fearful of the encroaches of the World the Flesh and the Devil upon his young men unless he held them in tight rein. Now he began to relax. Removed from the pseudo-monastic atmosphere he had tried to create in the Church Hostel and St. Michael's College, moving in the more normal world of a parish and responding to his parishioners as they responded to him, he rapidly shed the former tension and suspicion and became more human. He changed the parish, and the parish changed him.

The Standing Liturgical Commission of the Church in Wales started work in 1951 and Glyn was the first chairman. The call for liturgical revision had come from the Nation and Prayer Book Commission, set up in 1947, but Glyn did not think very much of the report it presented. He hoped that the members of the Liturgical Commission had read it "carefully and with discrimination", but they were not bound by it. His own ideas on liturgical revision were more cogent. It was a time of liturgical confusion and disobedience, based not upon theological principles but on purely utilitarian grounds, "due to a feeling, largely inarticulate, that the Liturgy of the Church (namely the 1662 Prayer Book) does not enable God's people to worship him and to hear his word as it did in the sixteenth and still more in the seventeenth centuries". He went on to say, in words which were significant for future developments : "We have also to take account of the Prayer Book in Welsh . . . I was once attacked in the Governing Body for saying that the Church in Wales has never really had a Prayer Book of its own ; but I am unrepentant ; in a strict sense I do not think it ever has." The procedure adopted was to produce revised services for an experimental period. It was confidently assumed that after a given period the final form of those services could be drawn up ; and it was hoped that in about twenty-five years the Church in Wales would possess a Prayer Book indisputably its own. The progress of liturgical revision has been more complex than was then supposed, and already the words "definitive versions" (presuming the need for further change) are being used instead of "final forms".

By the time the first of the experimental services came before the Governing Body. Glyn was no longer the chairman of the Liturgical Commission. He was the Bishop who had the responsibility for liturgical revision. As such he moved the second reading of the bill authorising the use of "revisions provisionally approved by the Bench of Bishops of the Book of Common Prayer" in 1954. This was the first of many speeches he was to make on this subject of which the object was, in his own words : "how best to enable that part of his Church, in which God has set us, to praise and honour him ; and to add her special part of the Liturgy, the bounden duty and service of the One Holy Catholic Apostolic Church throughout the world through whom the ' voice of prayer is never silent, nor dies the strain of praise away.' "

5

SWANSEA AND BRECON

1. The Bishop

One of Glyn's friends asked a cleric of the diocese of Swansea and Brecon how his new bishop was getting on. "Just as you would expect," was the reply, "poking his nose into everything and upsetting everybody." Glyn had been consecrated Bishop of Swansea and Brecon on the Feast of the Epiphany 1954. The service took place at Brecon because the Archbishop's Cathedral at Llandaff was still in the process of restoration. It was a splendid occasion and one which earned some commendation from a learned friend who wrote : "Let me congratulate you on the splendour of your consecration ; some of the details were shocking but the overall appearance and general run of the function were superb." Glyn was determined to wear dalmatic, tunicle and chasuble. Archbishop John Morgan, always a stickler for correctness (and the 1662 book was still the official Prayer Book of the Church in Wales), insisted on a rochet ; so Glyn wore a sleeveless rochet beneath the vestments which signified that the bishop summed up in himself the Ministry of the Church. The service books had been carefully annotated by John Morgan so that those taking part knew precisely what they should do ; while the lesser fry also knew that they would be decidedly upopular if they did not follow their instructions. Therefore the whole service for which the ancient Priory Church, the Cathedral of the new diocese, was the perfect setting, moved with faultless precision to its conclusion. The Bishop of Oxford, Kenneth Kirk, preached a magnificent sermon which was later published in the volume which took its title from that sermon, *Beauty and Bands*.[10]

Created in 1923 and carved out of the old diocese of St. Davids, Swansea and Brecon comprises the Archdeaconry of Brecon (the erstwhile counties of Breconshire and Radnorshire) and a new Archdeaconry of Gower (the City of Swansea and its environs). Edward Latham Bevan, then suffragan bishop of Swansea, was chosen to be its first bishop, but there seems to have been some opposition to his appointment because he could not speak Welsh. When the bishops met in synod to ratify the election, Archbishop Edwards refused to cast his vote, and he wrote trenchantly on the subject of language in Wales in the *Times* on the very day of Bevan's enthronement. But one wonders whether Edwards' motives were as altruistic as has generally been supposed, for Glyn thought that Edwards had a rather ambivalent attitude to Welsh.

It was never possible to predict how this would work out from time to time. I recall some incidents that suggest that Edwards really had little heart for the Welsh language (unlike his brother H. T. Edwards, Dean of Bangor). I remember an ordinand of the diocese of St. Asaph being interviewed by the Clerical Education Committee. He was a native of the Vale of Clwyd and questions revealed that he spoke no Welsh. Edwards leaned over towards the nervous youth and in his most winning way (and his charm could be very great) he asked him a couple of questions, ending with "And you don't speak Welsh ?" "No, sir," said the youth, obviously nervous of the effect of this answer on his chances. Judge his surprise, shared by the committee, at the next and final question : "Tell me then, how did you escape it ?" He said once to me, speaking in a llais bach bach which he used when wanting people to think of him as a very aged man : "You are young and I am old ; I would say just this one thing to you—learn Welsh." I recounted his conversation to Bishop Lloyd, his assistant bishop. "Well," he said, "on this very spot a few days ago he said to me : ' Welsh, Lloyd, the last refuge of the uneducated '."

Edwards did not disguise the fact that he thought little of Bevan but the reasons would seem to be personal rather than linguistic. Only towards the end of his time at St. Asaph did he invite Bevan to preach at the Cathedral. Afterwards he remarked to Glyn that he had been wrong all the time and said: "Bevan is a great man."

In his own diocese Bevan was greatly loved. He was much concerned with the new Cathedral and the precincts are, in a sense, his memorial ; for the old monastic buildings, then in private hands, were recovered during his time. He died in 1934 and endowed the Cathedral with the greater part of his personal fortune. Edwards died three years later and Glyn states that "The Province learnt to its surprise that of his estate of £30,000 he had left nothing to the Church in which he started his career as a penniless curate."

The election of John Morgan, then Rector of Llandudno, as Bevan's successor seems to have come as a surprise to the Province. He and Glyn became great friends in their Llandaff days but the friendship was not without its ups and downs. It was in one of the "downs" that Glyn snapped to his curate : "John Morgan, nobody had heard of him until he became secretary of the Bangor Patronage Board."

When John Morgan became Bishop of Swansea and Brecon, Glyn wrote, he naturally turned to his diocesan, C. A. H. Green, for advice and support :

> In the result the complete Green episcopal regimen was taken almost wholly over to Swansea and Brecon, files, regulations, directions, secret telephone—everything. They were already looking out of date even in Bangor. Nevertheless to Brecon they went and were applied vigorously. Bishop Bevan kept few files and fewer records of his diocese. He had it all, as it were in his head. John Morgan was a first class administrator with a streak of ruthlessness which apparently brought back memories to his school fellows of a pretty grim school prefect called "John Cop", a reference to his red hair.

Morgan was a man of great personal charm : "He had a real gift of friendship but only a select few were able to enjoy it ; many of the laity did and he enjoyed from them at all times of his life something approaching devotion." But he was a martinet and he had the fierceness which sometimes accompanies red hair and short stature. The clergy learned to tread delicately in his presence and it was not long before many stories were in circulation about the new bishop's ways and disciplines. Bishop Bevan had worn a cope and mitre and was not averse to the spectacular, but he was not interested in the niceties of ceremonial nor overcareful about correctness in procedure. John Morgan brought dignity and correctness into all that he did. The parish priest was left in no doubt as to what was required when the bishop came to his parish ; but, Glyn continues :

His weakest points were the rages he was apt to get into if anything went wrong at Confirmation, Ordination, or other services. There could be, too, an exasperating pernicketiness about small points. His own standards of accuracy and order were so high that he found it difficult to understand carelessness or other slips. Many clergy were "astonied" and even quite important dignitaries were "brought very low". My father, to whom Bevan had been a perfect bishop, did not much care for his successor and had, so far as I can remember, more than one brush with him. He had ignored some direction concerning the Confirmation and the bishop called his attention to it in the vestry after the service. "My Lord," he said, "I was presenting candidates for Confirmation when you were still in the cradle." But not all clergy were as courageous as my father, and the bishop's visit, with its unpredictable accompaniments, became something of a terror.

John Morgan was a hard taskmaster but he also worked hard himself. In 1938, again folowing Green's example, he reintroduced the Bishop's Visitation, a happening which only those clergy who were in Orders before 1900 could remember. Many documents were hastily signed before presentation to the diocesan whose eagle eye detected in almost every case the freshness of the ink. Morgan was translated to Llandaff in 1939 and E. W. Williamson, then Warden of St. Michael's College was elected to succeed him. His sudden death in September 1952 deprived the Province of a shy but saintly bishop and an eminent scholar.

The news of Glyn's election was received in the diocese of Swansea and Brecon with mixed feelings to say the least. One of the diocesan electors had publicly alleged that he was "too much of a schoolmaster". One of his friends used to refer to him at this time not, as the Constitution of the Church in Wales would have it, as the "bishop elect" but as the "bishop suspect". But a pleasant surprise awaited those who had only known him before he went to the parish of Llandaff. They were to discover that their new bishop wished to be not a pedagogue but a pastor. Such was his view of the bishop's office. It was primarily a pastoral one but the word "pastoral" needed to be carefully interpreted, as he wrote a few years later :

Hours of prayer will not excuse a Christian for not paying his bills or answering his letters. The office and work of a bishop involves not only the care of souls, spiritual leadership and liturgy ; it involves also the "care of the churches", and however rightly a bishop may delegate work, he will not be any more the spiritual man if he shirks administrative details, is careless about the finance or buildings of his diocese or leaves all committee work to others . . . I shall always be grateful to the late Dr. Kirk for the way in which he made it clear in the sermon he preached at my Consecration at Brecon Cathedral that the administrative responsibilities of a bishop are not merely a tiresome appendix to his pastoral work but "give him as full opportunities of loving and leading his people as the more congenial occasions when he opens his heart to them in the pulpit or in the pastoral letter".[11]

Kirk had spoken of the "beauty" of pastoral ministrations in the bishop's life, and also of the "bands" of administrative cares ; but the latter were to be regarded not as hindrances to direct pastoral activities but their essential concomitants. He also said that the bishop is "the fixed point in the diocese around which everything revolves" ; and this is what Glyn was determined to be.

A wind of change, or at least a gentle breeze, blew through the diocese. Candidates for ordination received the Bishop's personal attention. The clergy were invited to Ely Tower and their wives were charmed by Sheila Simon who carried them off to "see what had been done about the kitchen". Old vicarages were replaced, at least as many as money would allow without putting the Parsonage Board completely into liquidation. Glyn was still impatient of red tape and archdeacons were sometimes put out by his lack of respect for committee procedure or the need for a quorum. Visits to parishes became opportunities for the Bishop to make personal contact with his people, and his knowledge of what was going on in the diocese was quite phenomenal. It is said that when occasion required the Bishop to be a judge, he could be stern, even harsh, but in general he exuded a cheerfulness and friendliness which has long been remembered by both clergy and laity. He also struck a note of informality, symbolized by a stout refusal to wear gaiters, and by the sight of children from the local school (which his sons and daughter attended) playing cricket on the lawn of Ely Tower, formerly inhabited by his bachelor predecessors.

Glyn believed that a bishop should not be afraid to comment boldly on the events of the day. In a sermon for the Florence Nightingale Commemoration he called attention to "the conditions in Out-Patients Departments in many hospitals, the dreary surroundings, the impersonal atmosphere, and the long and often pointless waiting". These remarks did not pass without criticism, but he was gratified to find, a few months later, that the Minister of Health had asked for a review of the working of these departments. At his first Diocesan Conference he was critical of the Government over the invasion of Suez :

> We have been among the nations which most genuinely supported the United Nations. By so doing we openly committed ourselves to the principle that war is outmoded as a method of settling disputes. This great country . . . must persist to the very end, and even beyond it, in consultation and actions which will carry the support of the general conscience. We belong to a great nation ; and one of the marks of national greatness is the power to adapt ourselves to changing circumstances and times.

Suez was a sensitive subject. Aware that some of his hearers were not pleased, Glyn justified himself by a statement in his quarterly leaflet :

> We have not had in our actions the support of the general conscience of mankind ; and we are no longer strong enough in material power to impose our will on others. Without oil we are helpless ; and of all countries we are the most vulnerable to atomic weapons. Christian leaders ought to make these facts as clear as possible and to go on to emphasise that our history, and by and large our actions in recent years, can still secure for us true greatness in the moral realm, and opportunities for leadership of the world such as we have never had before. But these opportunities will depend upon our grasp of what our power in the world today really consists in, and on an unassailable integrity in international affairs.

But at the end of the leaflet was the note : "Confirmations are subject to rearrangement in consequence of the petrol shortage."

In 1956 he held his Primary Visitation. In the published Charge, however, he stated that whereas a bishop was required by Canon Law to hold a visitation every three years, "the Canonical requirements about visitations may be said to have been outmoded and to be no longer strictly relevant to the circumstances of today. It is unlikely that I shall carry out another visitation for five years, if I am spared that long, and it will not be so searching a one as this." Regarding the services of the Church he remarked: "We in this diocese have departed far from the primitive and Prayer Book ideal of a weekly act of worship centred on the Word and Sacrament ; in very few parishes is this service (the Eucharist) the best attended . . . This means that the centre of gravity of Church life in the diocese is wrong ; our worship is unsacramental and unsupernatural and therefore much weaker than it ought to be." He hoped that the clergy and laity would turn their minds to this matter and to consider how it might be remedied. The directions regarding the Occasional Offices are not without interest, for the influences of the modern world were beginning to impinge upon the discipline of an earlier age, for example marriages in Lent : "We cannot refuse to solemnise them but we are entitled to require that the service be as plain and simple as possible. Marriages in Holy Week are specially unsuitable, but modern conditions have made it necessary to relax our discipline as far as Holy Saturday is concerned." At this point the erstwhile chairman of the Liturgical Commission reasserted himself : "Answers to the Articles of Enquiry reveal that the Occasional Offices are now the least satisfactory part of the Book of Common Prayer and we look forward to proposals for their revision and improvement."

There are some typical "Simonisms", for example on churchyards : "Modern sentiment has turned, wrongly I think, against the best of all keepers of churchyard grass, and sheep may no longer safely graze amongst the expensive flowers and costly marbles which now mark man's last resting place" : or on the Church : "She must adapt her organisation and her system, as she must reinterpret the Faith, to changing circumstances, opportunities and needs, or be left stranded on the shores of Time, an object of affectionate curiosity to antiquarians but of tiresome irrelevance to everyone else." Indeed the Charge is still an interesting little document, as much for the assessment of the conditions of the time as for the reminder of the changes that have already taken place.

Glyn described himself in 1957 as a "stay-at-home" bishop, his life being bounded by diocese and province. He took a keen interest in local matters and was constantly in touch with his Member of Parliament, the present Lord Watkins, on these and on social matters. The saga of Ship Street, Brecon, is best told in his own words.

> Here in the sacred name of modern traffic it was proposed to demolish most of the houses on the left hand side. The obvious solution was to by-pass the town but nobody seems to have thought seriously of this. Those who began to were almost immediately put off by a dark warning from the Ministry of Transport that this would involve the building of a bailey bridge over the Usk which, they said, might well be there for years and years. Breconians shrank from the prospect. With two others I wrote to the Press ; we called in the Fine Arts Commission, the Council for the Preservation of Rural Wales, the Ministry of Housing and Local Government, the Ministry of Works and the County Planning Officer ; and representatives of these bodies met at Ely Tower. The Fine Arts Commission agreed to ask for an understanding from the Ministry of Transport that not more than four very dilapidated houses should be removed. Not only four but several charming houses have gone . . . Thus out of unimaginative parsimony and local indifference—"only a few old houses"—began the policy of destruction by nibble of one of the few towns in Wales with a distinctive character.[12]

He had already made his mark on one small matter as a leader in the revolt against the conventional attire of Anglican dignitaries. He refused to wear gaiters either at Lambeth meetings or anywhere else. Archbishop John Morgan was a stickler in these matters and on one occasion he tried to get the Archbishop of Canterbury to rebuke Glyn for being improperly dressed ; but Dr. Fisher contented himself by saying, "naughty man !" "I have the support of the Bishop of Birmingham," (J. L. Wilson) said Glyn, to which Fisher replied : "But he is always a rebel."

Archbishop Morgan died in 1957 and Glyn succeeded him as Bishop of Llandaff. The first episcopate was therefore brief but formative in many ways, not the least in one matter which involved him in controversy soon after he left Brecon.

2. THE PATRIOT

The zeal for Wales and the Welsh language which Glyn revealed in 1957 took some people by surprise, but it was no sudden phenomenon. Glyn and his sisters had been brought up to speak only English. Their parents were thoroughly Welsh but they belonged to a generation which spoke English at home, lapsing into the mother tongue only when they did not want the children to understand. Glyn's mentors at Brecon were all Englishmen and therefore Oxford and Crewe seemed hardly foreign to him. In short the Welsh language had no significance as far as his upbringing was concerned.

At Bangor he was none too patient with students who came from a completely Welsh background ; and some prospective ordinands remember that they were told to go home and learn English. But he provided Welsh services in the Hostel chapel and later, both at Bangor and Llandaff, he regularly took Welsh services himself. He had discovered that Welsh was not just a picturesque anachronism or a nuisance but a living language with its own distinctive culture ; and in the Senior Common Room of the University College he moved for the first time among scholarly Welshmen who were heirs to a tradition which previously he had not encountered. The Bangor years were formative. A new attitude to Welsh was developing even though it took a while to mature.

His criticism of the Gorsedd in 1950, while at first sight it seems to indicate a lack of sympathy with one of the chief vehicles of Welsh culture, in reality shows a growing interest and awareness of the problems of Wales in the modern age. On 14 November Glyn addressed the Monmouth Diocesan Conference, and in the course of his speech on the work of the Church he threw out a typical aside regarding the Gorsedd, the assembly of bards who officiate at the chief events of the (now Royal) National Eisteddfod. Earlier in the year, on 15

June, the Gorsedd had assembled at Llanrwst to proclaim the 1951 Eisteddfod. On this occasion Cynan, the new Archdruid, was installed. Glyn had this occasion in mind when he said :

> The Archdruid seems to be modelled on the Archbishop. He is enthroned with a kind of liturgy, wearing mitre and stole, and there are prayers and hymns and the pronouncement of a blessing. Few take these things very seriously, least of all the members of the Gorsedd, but in these vague and "groping" times, this kind of religiosity is a dangerous thing.

This was duly reported in the *Western Mail* and a few days later Cynan's reply was published. He poured scorn on the criticism made by the Dean of Llandaff and referred to the "regrettable ignorance of Welsh bardic history" on the part of one who "is not a member of the Gorsedd and does not even speak its language". He castigated Glyn's attitude as being that of the "clerigwyr Eingl" (English clergy) recalling the days of the English bishops who had borne rule in the past in Wales. A few letters to the editor kept the interest going until 28 November when it was announced that the Dean's reply would be published on the following day. It more than lived up to whatever expectation was aroused.

> In his recent outbursts the Archdruid suggests that I have been attacking the Eisteddfod. What I was dealing with was something quite different—the Gorsedd and its latest developments—and evidently I touched a very sensitive spot.
>
> The reason for this sensitiveness is perfectly plain—it is that the whole thing is a complete fraud. No one objects to a hymn and a prayer at the Eisteddfod, but the trouble is that they have been made part of a ceremony which is a fake from beginning to end. No one reading the Llanrwst Proclamation Booklet could guess—nor is he meant to—that what we are presented with is an 18th Century forgery with 19th Century additions, given a vague kind of religious setting which to some seems like a parody of Christian rites and to come near to blasphemy, by the suggestion that the "Bards of the Isle of Britain" have got hold of some kind of special revelation preserved in the Nod Cyfrin, and by the invocation of God's Name over all sorts of objects.
>
> Then there is all the pseudo-antique bric-a-brac, from the fake idioms and the circlet (which the Archdruid thinks I believe to be a mitre) through the ring (last year's addition, I

think) to the fetching little bootees whose date I have not traced. What pompous nonsense it all is and how much better for the Eisteddfod that it should diasappear altogether.

But human vanity will see that it does not and perhaps it is just as well, for we should lose a picture of singular piquancy. We should no longer see Church dignitaries cheek by jowl with Nonconformist divines, arrayed in ancient British robes as imagined by a 19th Century artist of modest powers, taking part in a ceremony invented by an 18th Century Unitarian literary forger, muttering blessings and indulging in a kind of liturgical patter arranged by a 20th Century Nonconformist minister of ritualistic tendencies.

Most people, the members of the Gorsedd in particular, were aware of the dubious history of that institution. Indeed, Glyn's ideas on the subject were not entirely his own. The original remark that sparked off the controversy had been put into his mind by one who was very close to Gorsedd circles ; and the letter to the *Western Mail*, and another to *Y Faner*, had been worked out in consultation with others who were equally close to the bards. But fact and fantasy can become inextricably mixed up in some minds which do not then like to be reminded of reality. Glyn was to see the logical consequence of this state of mind at the Investiture of the Prince of Wales in 1969, when, he remarks, "the proceedings received a somewhat bizarre touch by the appearance of two ' druidic ' figures, who were there, however, in their capacity as Free Church Ministers". Certainly their bardic robes appeared more splendid than those of the three bishops who accompanied them. But Glyn's criticism of the Gorsedd was that of an Anglo-Catholic who saw Church dignitaries (some of whom were decidedly evangelical) and Nonconformist ministers wearing "vestments" and enjoying a complicated "ceremonial" within the Gorsedd circle, when he knew that they regarded the traditional vestments and ceremonial of the Church as something akin to idolatry.

Glyn was Bishop of Swansea and Brecon when the Eisteddfod came to Ystradgynlais in 1954. He was therefore interested in this national event which was taking place in his diocese, and he hoped to receive an invitation to appear on the platform at the opening ceremony. But no invitation was forthcoming. The bards had not forgiven him for his devastating onslaught in the *Western Mail*, and no doubt the references to the "fetching little bootees" and such like still rankled. In the diocese a council of war was hastily summoned, an event which would have been lost to history had not the prime mover, J. L. Thomas, then vicar of Cockett, taken his curate, the Reverend Roswell M. Davies, with him to be a silent witness to the day-long consultation which took place at Ystradgynlais Rectory. With them was Dr. Maurice Jones and his support was decisive. He was then a very old man and there was some fear that the robes which were worn for the Gorsedd procession would be too heavy for his now frail frame. Maurice Jones was heard to say that his first duty was to the Church rather than the Gorsedd, and that he would not appear if the bishop of the diocese were not to be invited. Word was conveyed along the "grapevine" to this effect with the result that a seat was found for Glyn on the platfrom, but so perilously close to the edge that he was in mortal danger of going over the side. This was a lesson which was not forgotten.

His circle of friends included a number of men who were prominent both in the life of the Church and the Nation. Also his wife, Sheila, was thought to be becoming increasingly nationalistic in outlook. They helped him to become aware of a growing Welsh consciousness which could not be ignored. He found parishes in the Swansea valley where Welsh was flourishing, and he entered as fully as possible into their life. In his first Visitation Charge he had a good deal to say about the Welsh Language. The Articles of Enquiry had revealed that there was a considerable amount of Welsh spoken in the diocese: "162 chapels and 42 churches have services in Welsh ; when we remember that the 162 is divided amongst three or four different religious bodies the Church proportion seems about right". There was evidence, however, that there were many cases where the maintenance of Welsh services was difficult owing to the decline of the use of the language by the young. Glyn thought that the new Welsh schools might change this : "In these schools lies the chief hope of the preservation of the Welsh language . . . It would be disastrous indeed if the Church (which is the heir in this land of the Welsh Saints) which saved the language and thereby Welsh nationality at the Reformation, should now be found wanting."

Here he was repeating some of the things he had said in a broadcast talk (later published) in his Cardiff days when he had read both Welsh and English-speaking churchmen some lessons in decorum. He had bidden the first "to escape from a narrow parochialism, often essentially nonconformist, into a wider vision of the Church Catholic" ; and he had reminded the second that "the Church's duty to the people of Wales is not ended by voting a small subisdy to *Y Llan* ; nor is it enough to smile tolerantly when a Welsh accent is heard on the platform at Cardiff or Llandrindod". Rather it was the task of the Church to help in the work of unity, "and solve the problem of tongues in the possession of a common faith". His zeal for Wales and the Welsh language was, therefore, no sudden phenomenon, as seems to have been thought by some at least of the members of the Electoral College when they assembled at Llandrindod 5 November 1957 to choose a new Archbishop.

By this time Glyn had already been translated to the diocese of Llandaff and his successor as Bishop of Swansea and Brecon had been appointed. This was J. J. A. Thomas, the then Arch-deacon of Gower, one of the best loved and one of the more distinguished sons of the Church in Wales ; but one who by the accident of birth had been brought up in the English-speaking area of Pembrokeshire. Then on 5 November, the Electoral College chose the Bishop of Monmouth, Alfred Edwin Morris, as the new Archbishop. After his retirement and not long before his death he commented wrily : "I was the first English-man to become Archbishop of Wales, and probably I shall also be the last."

Glyn and the new Archbishop were men of different temper-ament, the one a complex and volatile (perhaps Welsh) charac-ter, the other, as Glyn saw him, "an Englishman through and through" :

Tall, handsome, upright, courageous, energetic and very hard working, strong willed and conscious of his powers. He was reserved, perhaps rather shy, and it was not possible to get near him. He was a man who walked alone and preferred it so. Another side of his nature was revealed to those who knew him well. I was not among them but discovered this in another way. He had to spend some time in Llandough Hospital and I called in to see him. His wife was in the ward when I came. I was immediately aware of his devotion to her, changing and softening the somewhat stern lines of his face.

Glyn had a good deal of respect for Morris's ability. Indeed his only criticism is that Morris seemed to be unaffected by the "winds of change".

He was a good theologian and argued his proposals and statements from firm theological bases. This is not very common among bishops today. I remember an occasion when the English bishops were discussing the service of Benediction and other undesirable goings-on. Morris happened to be sitting next to me and he remarked : "These people have no theology at all : they are arguing from a purely pragmatic standpoint."

In the age of "Documentary Christianity" Glyn was tempted to pay little heed to the showers of documents which descended on the bishops.

I was confident that I could rely on Morris for a useful, well-balanced and theologically informed summary of these. Vengeance fell on me when I succeeded him as Archbishop, for my reluctance, indeed my inability, to give these various documents the study that was essential, while attempting to run a large diocese at the same time, were certainly factors in my having to give up office so much sooner than I expected.

But he continued : "Archbishop Morris possessed, again in common with his fellow-countrymen, other qualities of a kind which led them to be unaffected by the ' winds of change ', a phrase whose inventor was half English and half Celtic." One of the things Glyn had in mind was the Welsh language in which Morris seemed to take little interest. But he immediately goes on to say, in fairness to Morris, that the College he served for so many years was, in the words of one of its Welsh-speaking *alumni*, "not a Welsh college at all, it was merely a college in Wales" ; and the country which Morris knew as a younger man was not very language conscious.

It has been revealed from Morris's unpublished memoirs

that he began to learn Welsh in 1924 but he was put off by those who should have encouraged him :

> When it became known that I had begun to learn Welsh, one ardent Welshman commented that he supposed that Morris was aiming to become a Welsh bishop . . . The innuendo wounded me so deeply that I resolved there and then that I would never lend any colour to it, and I at once dropped my attempt to learn Welsh. Perhaps I was over-sensitive . . . but the thought of being suspected of scheming to use the Welsh language to aid an ambition which seemed to me to be wrong in itself—since no man ought to seek to become a bishop—was so distasteful that I could not endure it.[13]

But in Glyn's case the winds of change did not begin to blow till long after that time.

Glyn went to the Electoral College determined not to let his name go forward and to use his influence on behalf of one of the Welsh-speaking bishops. But in a weak moment and under pressure from his friends he did not oppose his nomination. This was a mistake and it weakened his position in the controversy which followed the appearance of the Llandaff Diocesan Leaflet in January 1958. Glyn's crtiicism was really aimed at the Electoral College. He tried to make it clear that no personal attack was intended, but not everyone, least of all the Archbishop, could accept this rather fine distinction. On the one hand Glyn wrote : "The new Archbishop and the new Bishop of Swansea and Brecon are, it goes without saying, men of academic distinction and personal piety, ' godly and well-learned men ' as the Prayer Book says bishops ought to be ; and we wish them all blessings and will keep them constantly in our prayers as they go about their high work." On the other hand he referred to the two elections as "a severe blow to the confidence of many Welsh-speaking Church folk" and he went on to say that "the recent elections, and utterances before and after them, have revealed an anti-Welsh and pro-English bias, and in some cases a bigotry as narrow and ill-informed as any to be found in the tightest and most remote Welsh communities".

The news media rejoiced in this source of copy. It was quoted on the radio and even the *Church Times* took note of what its correspondent called "Pro-English Trends in Welsh Elections", while the editor dilated on "The Welsh Feud". Glyn urged a number of his friends to write to that paper saying that "there is no feud in the Church in Wales but there is a sense of nationhood". But it was of no avail. The editor failed to find space for them. The annoyance felt by Glyn and his friends is reflected in the words of Theomemphus, the pseudonym of Aneirin Talfan Davies, who wrote a pamphlet called *Bilingual Bishops and All That* which Glyn read before publication.

> We believe that the intervention of the Editor of the *Church Times* in this controversy deserves at least a mention. Under the patronizing and superior heading, "The Welsh Feud", he proceeds to read the Welsh churchmen who criticised the Electoral College's decision a lesson in pious decorum. Whilst feeling himself free to indulge in gratuitous comment, the Editor nevertheless saw fit to ignore the letters of leading Welsh clergymen and laity, and this prevented readers from assessing the true facts of the so-called "feud".

Glyn was being singled out for attack in other quarters so that Theomemphus was moved to defend him :

> It is worth noting in the present controversy that it was precisely those who were antipathetic to the Welsh language who introduced the personal element. The Bishop of Llandaff in his Diocesan Leaflet makes it clear that no personal attack on the Archbishop was intended . . . Any reading of the Bishop's *full* statement would, in any civilised community, have saved him from attacks upon his integrity and honesty. It was a very difficult statement for any bishop to have made at such a time, and it could only have been the realisation of the supreme importance of the acts of the Electoral College for good or for ill which could have persuaded him to make it. This in itself should have been enough to protect him from the bitter and uncharitable personal attacks he has had to suffer.

But, in fact, those who took part in the controversy were very few. Aneirin ap Talfan's pamphlet had been given wide publicity but its circulation was very small. It was difficult to argue the matter on principle only, without involving personalities, and that the vast majority of Welsh churchmen were not prepared to do.

After showing his hand in the Diocesan Leaflet, Glyn took no further part in the public controversy ; but his postbag was all the heavier for it. There was some correspondence with the Archbishop whom he invited to pay an official visit to the diocese of Llandaff. Morris, probably the last Archbishop who spurned the typewriter and wrote his own letters in longhand, replied :

> To be quite frank, I do not think I could happily pay an official visit to your diocese at present. You have told the world, in effect, that you think I am not qualified to be Archbishop of Wales, and I do not see how you could welcome me as Archbishop.

Glyn protested that his objections were made in principle and that no personal criticism was intended : "I do not object to Edwin Morris as Archbishop ; I object in principle to an Archbishop who has no knowledge of the Welsh tongue in a bilingual Province." But this was a distinction too fine for the Archbishop to accept. Glyn solved the problem by inviting him to preach at a service at Llandaff Cathedral to mark the opening of the Empire Games. This was an invitation that Morris found he could accept "without compromising my position and without embarrassment to either of us".

Glyn had many letters of support but there were others which took him to task for his own lack of Welsh, reminding him that it had been said at the Electoral College : "If Monmouth goes to the National Eisteddfod as Archbishop, he will have to keep his mouth shut ; if Llandaff goes, he may open his mouth and put his foot in it." Glyn replied that he had never claimed to be Welsh-speaking and had gone out of his way to make this plain both at the Governing Body and the Electoral College.

The Bishop of St. Davids, J. R. Richards, attempted to pour oil on troubled waters. He pointed out that he and others like him were not actuated by anti-Welsh motives when they voted as they did in the previous elections. He continued :

> I feel very strongly that both the new Archbishop and the new Bishop of Swansea and Brecon have as much right to consider their election as manifestly the Will of God, as you or I in the

matter of our elections. I am not prepared to believe that after the election to Llandaff the Holy Ghost ceased to guide the minds of those called to serve on the Electoral College.

The letter found Glyn in an intractable mood. He thanked the Bishop for it, remarked that he had been half expecting it, and added that he agreed with nothing in it :

> I cannot share your views about the Electoral College and the guidance of the Holy Spirit, and I certainly do not hold, as you suggest I do, that your election and mine were manifestly the Will of God, and that the Holy Spirit was guiding the Electoral College when we were elected and ceased to guide it in the case of the last two elections. I am by no means certain that God meant me to come here. The election was swift and decisive and that influenced my decision. But only time will tell whether it was due or not to the Holy Spirit. This claiming of plenary inspiration, or even infallibility, for the Electoral College seems to be exactly covered by Bishop Butler's words to John Wesley : "This is a very horrid thing, Sir, a very horrid thing."

On the other issues Glyn remarks that it was more than just a matter of speaking Welsh :

> A case can be made out for the bilingual Welsh clergy being the strongest anglicising influence we have ; and Saunders Lewis says somewhere that Wales had no greater foes than Welsh-speaking Welshmen. It is a matter of knowing something of the history and the ethos of Wales, and being familiar with leading Welshmen of today, and knowing something of the new situation which has developed with the revival of Welsh in the last quarter of a century. The Electoral College does not begin to be aware of this.

Thus the letter brings us back to the Electoral College, that body to which Glyn stood in a kind of love-hate relationship. After his retirement he wrote :

> People who elect bishops in Wales are for the most part the same (clergymen in particular) as serve on the various committees and commissions which do much valuable work for the Church. This, however, is the making of such beings to be conservative and to wish, almost at any cost, to avoid rows, or being made to feel uncomfortable through newspaper articles and the publicity which goes with such. They prefer to do their good deeds by stealth, to damp down any opposition at an early stage so as "not to get into the press".

71

The Electoral College is composed of the Archbishop and Bishops ; six clerical and six lay electors form the vacant See and three clerical and three lay electors from the other dioceses ; and the person who "receives two-thirds of the votes of those present and voting" is declared by the President to be the Bishop-Elect. Representative rather than democratic, for the electors are appointed by the Diocesan Conferences rather than by the whole body of the faithful—an ideal but impracticable method—the system is not perfect, but as Glyn was to insist, any mistakes made were the mistakes of the Church itself and not of a power outside it. When some criticism of the Electoral College was voiced in England he rose to its defence.

The criticism came from Carl Witton-Davies. He had come back to Wales from Jerusalem as Dean of St. Davids but he was now Archdeacon of Oxford. Speaking in the Canterbury Convocation on the appointment of bishops in general, he referred in passing to the Welsh system and remarked that there was a danger of lobbying in such a method of election. He had made the same point in a letter to the *Daily Telegraph* a few weeks before, but the sole intention was to suggest that no man-made system of appointing bishops was perfect. Glyn took these remarks as a personal affront—perhaps the Archdeacon had touched a tender spot—and he wrote a rather fierce letter to his former colleague.

> I am very grieved to read in today's *Church Times* that you have repeated some remarks about "lobbying" in our Electoral College which apparently you made some time ago in a letter to the *Daily Telegraph*. It does not seem to me decent that you should permit yourself to talk in this way about the Church in Wales to which you owe so much. Moreover, in my judgement, what you say is not true, and if it is, it is no less true of what happens in connection with appointments by the Prime Minister. I know a good deal more than you do about Electoral Colleges in Wales, and it is on the whole remarkable that they are so free from what you call "lobbying". I can think of only two elections where rather unedifying things happened, both long before your time . . . Quite a number of people resent your remarks and this leads to talk of "disappointed ambition" etc., which is a great grief to one who prepared you for Confirmation and worked with you so happily in days gone by.[14]

72

Brecon Cathedral from the east

Llandaff Cathedral: Pulpitum and Majestas

Witton-Davies drafted a lengthy reply but he decided not to send it. He would wait until he had the opportunity to speak personally to Glyn about these things. Had he sent the letter, Glyn would have read :

> Inevitably, reports of speeches do not convey the whole import of what the speaker has said . . . One newspaper made no mention of my references to the Church in Wales but simply reported the main point of my speech, that the appointing or electing of bishops is liable to abuse and criticism . . . The debate in the House of Clergy last week included references to similar situations in New Zealand and to experiences north of the Border. We were all simply stressing the fact that whether the English system survives as it is, or in a modified form, or whether there exists what on paper seems a more democratic method, all these systems have their objections.

He admitted that the candidates themselves were not parties to the lobbying, but he objected to "the eloquent speeches that can be made in support of candidates not known to the majority of electors who are then likely to be swayed". He had heard of one being described as "an eminent scholar of European stature", an instance when the fervour of the supporter was not matched by the accuracy of the description.

Later their correspondence took a more general turn when Witton-Davies was invited by the Archbishop of Canterbury to be a member of his "Crown Appointments Commission". Glyn remained obdurate in his distrust of the English method of appointing bishops. He was prepared to admit that it worked tolerably well but that was all.

> Briefly speaking, no method is infallible, but as things are at present, when mistakes are made in the appointment of bishops in the Church of England, they are not made by the Church which could learn from the experience but by a secular body outside the Church, though often, and latterly always, sympathetic to advice given by Church leaders.

Witton-Davies still had reservations about electoral systems of appointment such as obtained in the Church in Wales.

> Granted the key person is the Prime Minister's Appointments Secretary but anybody can find out who he is and approach him. This is, I admit, a counter argument to what I said

publicly in the House of Clergy and wrote in the columns of the *Daily Telegraph* three years ago. I still believe the possibility of lobbying, or "canvassing" as you call it, to be one of the grave weaknesses of the elective system. Much evidence we have had from other parts of the Anglican Communion than Wales has supported this|fear. But the English system is of course equally open to this possible objection, except that the method of activity would be slightly different.

More letters passed between them but neither could win the other to his point of view. Glyn finally summed the matter up in characteristic fashion.

English bishops are in theory appointed by the Sovereign (for which as the Sovereign is a *persona mixta* there is much to be said) ; in fact they are appointed by the Prime Minister, but this in turn is not the real situation. The appointment is really made by an anonymous person who appears to scamper round the Athenaeum and similar institutions, and to have recourse to a card index or list compiled on nobody knows what principles. I say he is anonymous but in fact all ambitious clergymen seem to know who he is. I hope you were fair to the Welsh system ; of course there are weaknesses ; no doubt there are mistakes ; no doubt there is, though not openly, "canvassing" on occassions. But at least all this is within the Church, which seems to be altogether better than a situation in which the mistakes made are sombody else's and not the Church's.

Despite the earlier reservations about the Electoral College of the Church in Wales, there would seem to be no better way, in Glyn's eyes, of appointing bishops.

Glyn's zeal for Wales and the Welsh language, developed at Brecon and manifested at Llandaff, was to continue unabated. He worked hard at Welsh and gained a considerable proficiency in it. His accent was never very pure but that did not worry him.

3. THE ECCLESIOLOGIST

In 1956 Glyn was invited to become President of the Ecclesiological Society in succession to W. R. Matthews, Dean of St. Paul's. The Society was but a shadow of its former self but its history was such that Glyn was attracted to it. Founded in 1839 as the Cambridge Camden Society it was refounded in

1845 as the Ecclesiological Society and through its journal, *The Ecclesiologist*, it exercised a dominating influence on church architecture, becoming almost the final arbiter in matters of taste and design during the period of the Gothic Revival. That a London-based society should look to Brecon for its new President also indicates that Glyn himself was becoming known in ecclesiological circles.

His interest in church architecture began when, as a boy, he had thumbed through the pages of *The Ecclesiologist*. It was stirred by his father's rebuilding of St. David's, Brecon, and by the building of the Hostel Chapel at Bangor which brought him into contact with H. L. North, an "art and craft" architect and author of *The Old Churches of Snowdonia* (1924). This book, and the works of E. Tyrrell-Green, showed him that the church architecture of Wales was worthy of serious study. Glyn had a high regard for Tyrrell-Green's books, and when he first met George Pace he was delighted to find another admirer of the same author.[15] His long association with Pace, not only in the rebuilding of Llandaff Cathedral but also in the care of many churches both in the dioceses of Swansea and Brecon and Llandaff, helped him to build up a considerable knowledge of architecture both ancient and modern.

The members of the Ecclesiological Society met their new President at a special meeting 26 November 1956 when he read a paper on the restoration of Llandaff Cathedral. In the following year he was the preacher at the annual festival, on that occasion held at Holy Trinity, Kensington, one of the churches designed by G. F. Bodley, the nineteenth century architect, who was being commemorated at the festival. Glyn spoke of the need to see all parts of a church and its furnishings "as parts which give significance to, and derive their significance from the one building whose purpose it is to set forth the glory of God in the supreme act of Christian worship". He was thinking, in particular, of what had been done in Llandaff Cathedral ; and George Pace has stated that Glyn "recognised the dangers of architects using the cliches of modern architecture and techniques without deep understanding and self-negation : he hated all shams and collections of current cliches : for such a church he had a name, ' St. Liquorice Allsorts ' ".

Bodley, Glyn declared, was one who exemplified what he was trying to say. There was a wholeness about his work as of a man who understood what he was about and where he was going. He designed churches as a setting for the Liturgy as it was understood in his day. "Our understanding of the Liturgy has changed and is changing", but still the task of the architect is to build a church "as an expression of the worship of the One True God, through the knowledge of him in Jesus Christ through his Holy Spirit."

In Bodley's day the Ecclesiological Society was a power in the land. Now it was in danger of becoming "a learned and limited society moving in its dignified way from church to church in the Metropolis, with occasional and equally dignified excursions beyond it". The Society could be still a power in the land if it succeeded in capturing the attention of young architects who were concerned with the problems of church building in the present day. It could play the part of the "faithful and wise steward, capable of bringing out of his treasures things both new and old, lucidly expounding the past, creatively criticising the present, and sustaining and informing the great art of church building". The Society was much concerned about its image and about its future. For that reason Glyn suggested (though it came to nothing) that it should become allied to the New Churches Research Group which was another of his interests.

In 1957 the Rector of Bagendon, Peter Hammond, invited a number of friends to a meeting to discuss the possibility of doing something about the dreadful "modern churches" which were beginning to spring up all over the country. Glyn and George Pace were soon involved and by 1958 it had become the New Churches Research Group with Glyn as President. It issued a manifesto which contained the statement: "We share with Spain and Ireland the unenviable distinction of being the only country in western Christendom which does not possess a single periodical devoted to the problem of church design." A symposium was planned, to be edited by Peter Hammond with a weighty preface by Glyn; but in the event the editor found it easier to write the book himself. During the next few years the Group attracted a good deal of support and branches were set up in New Zealand, Australia, Canada and elsewhere. By 1962 the character of the group had changed. The office of President was abolished and, in recognition of the interdenominational character that it now assumed, Glyn became one of a number of Patrons, remaining one of them until his death. But many of the members felt that the Group had served its purpose. Its mission had been prophetic ; now it was up to those involved in concrete situations to work out the implications of the prophecy.

Peter Hammond and Glyn appeared on television 17 June 1962 in a programme called "Why Cathedrals ?" They were both outspoken ; Hammond remarked that cathedrals had been a bad influence on parochial worship (because the parish church tried to ape the cathedral) ; Glyn said that the ancient cathedrals ought to be taken over by the Ministry of Works, and he questioned whether they had any impact on the tourist. They received many letters of protest and to one of these Glyn replied : "You are incorrect in describing me as ' anti-cathedral' ; what I am *anti* is cathedrals as they are too frequently organised at the present time ; and also *anti* the immense sums of money that have been spent on four new cathedrals in this country in recent years, three of these completed and one planned.[16] I believe we are the only country now building on this scale, and nobody could say it was because we were excessively religious." The programme roused great wrath among cathedral dignitaries and some hard words were said about it in the Church Assembly. Another programme was hastily arranged, but this time Glyn had to face the then Dean of Gloucester, S. J. A. Evans, who was put up more or less to defend the establishment. Two years before, Evans had written that Glyn's lecture to the Diocesan Advisory Committees' Conference at Oxford was the best thing they had heard for a long time. Now the Dean did the lecturing and Glyn said comparatively little ; but his silence was thought to be eloquent.

In his sermon at Kensington Glyn remarked that some of the mistakes of the ecclesiologists of the 19th Century had been disastrous, "not the least in Wales where the particular genius of the land and the local church patterns were completely missed". He developed this point in the closing remarks of

77

his presidential address to the Cambrian Archaeological Association in 1965 :

> There is our special heritage in Wales of hundreds and hundreds of little ancient churches. They are for the most part unknown, and come as a revelation to architects and lovers of the past who see them for the first time. They are quite different from any in England. They are small and simple and very much home-made. They fit the landscape and the climate ; they are the offerings of a poor people, harassed over the centuries by war and living on land very different from the rich rolling counties of England. Only rarely do we see churches comparable to any of the great churches over the border and when we do, we find that they are the offerings of Englishmen and carried out by English masons . . . Because our idiom is so different it is apt to be despised. Ecclesiologists last century described our churches, as "rude barn-like structures" and ruthlessly improved them by the insertion of arches and windows in the second pointed style, for them the last word in "correct" church architecture. For much the same reason a public authority in Wales declined to help a small country church with many interesting medieval features because it was "not of national importance"—the test of such importance apparently being one of size and grandeur . . . It seems to me that there is a real danger of making the same mistake about Welsh churches today as was made in a big way architecturally last century. The mistake is to judge them by English standards ; the Welsh scale of things, the traditions, the achievements, should all be judged from a quite different level from England, for everything is on a smaller scale, and the very poverty, small size and simplicity of many of our churches is part and parcel of our heritage.

He remarked that many county councils had recognised this heritage by making grants towards restoration and preservation from their Welsh Church Act Funds, that is the monies handed over to them under the Welsh Church (Disestablishment) Act : "But by no means all our county councils do this and there is much converting work to be done." Glyn was thinking in particular about Glamorgan County Council which in 1959 refused to make a grant towards the preservation of an important wall painting in Colwinston Church, despite the fact that they were given the opinion of a leading expert that the painting was unrecorded, of great importance and in real danger of perishing. The Council had decided to adhere to its policy whereby grants should be restricted to churches of national rather than local importance. Glyn tartly wrote : "One wonders on what basis and with what expert advice and knowledge this question of ' national importance' is decided"; and he continued :

> The great bulk of the visible history of Wales is enshrined in our numeruos small churches and nonconformist chapels (though the latter are necessarily many fewer). Set in our hills and valleys, they are built out of their stones and adorned by their timber, fashioned by rural craftsmen singularly gifted in the carving and enrichment of wood . . . They are part and parcel of our history, but, apparently, to the Glamorgan County Council they are of no national importance.[17]

He thought it sad that the county which should have given an enlightened lead had so far failed.

Glyn's appreciation of the vernacular qualities of Welsh church architecture was sharpened by long discussions with George Pace. They travelled extensively in the Archdeaconry of Brecon where they found many examples of indigenous churches, even though all too many of them had been "eviscerated", as Glyn used to say, by the 19th Century ecclesiologists. In later days when Glyn was chairman of the Churches Committee of the Representative Body of the Church in Wales, their discussions covered a much wider field. They both at different times proclaimed the need for something to be done which would be parallel to what the photographs of Edwin Smith, the writings of John Betjeman and the drawings of John Piper had done for English churches ; and Pace listed the things that such a portrait of Welsh churches and chapels should include :

> the stark campanili of Pembrokeshire and the west ; the moving simplicity of the interiors of remote one and two cell churches ; the spatial complexity of interiors arising out of plan forms almost unknown in England ; the many sub-regional groups of tower and bell turret design ; the external compositions producing visual and picturesque effects pre-eminently Welsh ; the superb rood screens of the Border ; the subtle relationship between design and materials and the land-

scape of various geological formations ; the assimilation of influences from adjoining countries into definitely Welsh forms ; the rude, vital and ecitixng minor crafts of all ages, in carvings, wall paintings, tombs, headstones and furnishings. We might expect to see the white washed exterior of Llanybri which would remind us of medieval Danish churches ; St. Govan's Chapel, overwhelmed by its vast rocks ; the stately local Perpendicular of Clynnog Fawr and Llywel ; the complex external forms of Llantwit Major, St. Mellon's and Coity ; the humbling atmosphere of Rhulen, Llanbadarn-y-Garreg, Llanfrynach or Disserth ; the tiny barn-like structure of Llanfihangel Helygen ; the great Jesse at Abergavenny ; the tombs of Llantrithyd ; the tabernacle work at Llancarfan; the rare rood figures at Kemeys Inferior and Mochdre ; but what we should expect to see is endless.

Nonconformist chapels form an important part of the corpus of Welsh ecclesiastical architecture, and our imagined book would show simple, unaffected and very moving chapels— Aberaeron, Rhydlwyd, Begelley and Llansadwrnen ; those architecturally orthodox—Llanon and Blaenconin ; and those that are architecturally astonishing—Bethesda, Tenby, Aber-aeron, Kilgetty and Pen-y-Bryn.[18]

These things were being said for the first time. They were and still are of the utmost importance.

Glyn's work in the care of Welsh churches did not pass unnoticed. It was on this account that in 1966 he was able to write himself a Fellow of the Society of Antiquaries. In the same year his old college recognised his maifold activities and he was elected to an honorary Fellowship of Jesus College.

6

LLANDAFF

1. HITHER AND THITHER

The new Bishop of Llandaff, enthroned 5 October 1957, had not been long in his diocese when he wrote in a letter : "The real bafflement comes in for me when I try to do my job as bishop." He could no longer describe himself as "a stay-at-home bishop". Outside engagements were increasing though some of them had been accepted before he left Brecon. These included a commentary in the Torch series on I Corinthians, a University Sermon at Cambridge, a paper at a Eucharistic Conference at the Albert Hall, and the joint secretaryship of the Bible Committee of the Lambeth Conference. So he wrote in the first issue of his Diocesan Leaflet : "If you do not see me much about the diocese during the first quarter of 1958 you must not think of me as taking things easy."

Soon he aquired another task, to edit the book, *Bishops*, which was published in 1961, and he gathered together a distinguished team to explain what those functionaries were and what they did. His own essay has been remembered in particular for his remarks about bishops' houses : "It is not enough that bishops should live simply ; they must be *seen* to live simply . . . Let the bishop live in a much smaller house, and let his office needs be seen and recognised for what they are, part of his official life which he cannot escape and which needs space in which to discharge it." There is no evidence, however, that he sought to practise what he preached. He used to say in those days that he had an assistant lecturer's stipend and ought to live in a similar kind of house. His Archdeacon, Gwynno James, lived in daily fear that someone would take him at his word and present him with a "semi-detached" in the suburbs.

The statement about bishops' houses is not the only provocative aside in the essay. He remarks upon the unsatisfactory nature of the prevailing position in England and Wales whereby the pastoral oversight of the Church is in the bishops' single and individual hands : "Anything less prelatical by nature than the average bishop in these Provinces it would be difficult to imagine, but anything more prelatical in fact and in effect than the way in which they exercise their *episcope* is not easy to picture." Then again he says : "Incidentally, when the Church of England makes much of episcopacy as the focus of unity, sceptical onlookers are apt to ask awkward questions." The influence of the other contributors on his thinking was considerable. Their ideas appear not infrequently in various talks and writings. In particular he was fascinated by John Robinson's "New Model of Episcopacy" and he thought of applying its principles to Wales. In his address to the Governing Body in 1970 he said : "We need something of the kind that Bishop Robinson advocated in the book on bishops which I edited a few years ago—a college of bishops in a diocese such as that of Llandaff, each with his own church and chair. This might give some chance of getting laity and clergy to recognise that what matters is not the presence of a diocesan bishop at their various rites and functions but the presence of a bishop."

The "Torch Commenatary" on I Corinthians was published in 1959. It is not a profound work nor was it meant to be. The writers in the Series, while taking the results of modern scholarship into account, were to be concerned with the Bible as the Word of God. With this object in mind, Glyn's little book contains a number of stimulating passages which endeavour to demonstrate the relevance of St. Paul to the present day. There are also a number of typical asides such as the comment : "It is the Apostle's misfortune that many who know nothing else about him have a vague idea that he was anti-feminist, liked women to have their hair long, and insisted on thhir having their heads covered in church." Therefore there were many, until quite recent times, "long after their religion had become vestigial, who were reluctant to enter a church building without putting a handkerchief or similar object on the heads of their women-folk".

At Cambridge Glyn preached on Christian Asceticism. The sermon shows that he was aware of changing circumstances but also saddened by the demise of earlier disciplines. In the past there had been much asceticism of a highly individualistic kind : "It is not surprising that with the deeper understanding we now have of the hidden springs of too many such practices, the 20th Century has witnessed a sharp reaction against asceticism of any kind." Here lay a danger "seen perhaps in much of the attitude of Anglican post-Tractarians towards Lent, in its deprecation of acts of self-denial, or the surrender of this or that pleasure or indulgence to which our fathers were so much given . . . Indeed we are told that we must practise a ' positive ' Lent, one that can go on just as usual but with more emphasis on prayer and the things of the spirit and so forth . . . This seems dangerously like the kind of spirituality which St. Paul so strongly denounced."

Then came the Lambeth Conference of 1958 and in August the Church Union held its Eucharistic Conference at the Albert Hall. At some point in the proceedings a standing ovation was given to a prominent Anglo-Catholic priest, already advanced in age, who was considered to have done much to foster devotion to Our Lady in this land. Glyn was still irritated if things became too "Roman" and he kept his seat. This required no little courage for he was Episcopal Vice-President of the Church Union and therefore seated on the platform. He read his paper and he too received a standing ovation. Sometime later Lord Wicklow wrote from Ireland : "Freddy Hood was over here and told me how you made easily the best speech at the Eucharistic Conference." One result was that Glyn was invited to the United States by the American Church Union. Sheila's health at this time was a matter of grave concern but she was able to accompany her husband on this visit and she enjoyed it to the full. They boarded the *Queen Elizabeth* 4 October 1962 ; but Sheila still retained the ideals of her youth for she looked at her surroundings and noted in the diary she kept at this time :

Staff very friendly everywhere ; stewards to tuck blankets— degrading job ; kind of thing that is almost Victorian : women mostly middle-aged ; pampered ; not forthcoming ; expensive clothes ; hair done to death ; signs of baldness all round.

In New York they were housed in the Savoy Hilton and welcomed with a banquet at which, Sheila noted, "G spoke very well". Glyn also had a conscience about the splendour of their surroundings when he wrote to his secretary, Mrs. Betty Horley, who was required to keep him informed of any matters of import in his diocese :

> As you will see from the notepaper, here we are till Friday, very unsuitably housed for a bishop. Where we go after Friday has not been revealed, but I have done my best to probe the charming but vague Du Bois into letting you know.

In the event they set off for Paoli in Pensylvania and Sheila's diary for the first Sunday reads : "Mass at 7-45 ; service at St. David's at 9.30, packed, lots of children, families together etc. ; 11 a.m. Parish Church, packed ; 3.30 leave for Philadelphia station for Washington." On the following Tuesday they were back in Philadelphia. They moved westwards to Cleveland, Toledo, Fort Wayne and Chicago. On 26 October they were travelling to New Hampshire. Visits to Baltimore and Boston followed and then back to New York which they left 16 November.

In the Diocesan Leaflet of April 1963 Glyn took stock of his activities :

> A somewhat unexpected problem in my episcopate has been the number of things I am asked to do outside the diocese and indeed outside the province. It is difficult to know what to do about these occasions, but this year, without realising it, I have become involved in rather too many of them. If I am spared next year, I propose to restrict outside engagements severely, the more so as Messrs Hodder and Stoughton have commissioned a book from me at the end of 1964.

The book was not written. The demands upon his time were too great and it was difficult to put his good intentions into practice. At the time of writing he was already committed to be one of the representatives of the Church in Wales at the Anglican Congress at Toronto in the following August. In November he was to lead a mission to the University of Durham.

When Glyn spoke at Toronto on ' Strategy in the Anglican

Communion', he urged the need for radical change. The last paragraph of his speech briefly sums up the whole :

> On all that I have been speaking of, some progress, often slow and hesitant, has been made. Greater unity within Anglicanism itself ; swifter progress from Anglo-Saxon to Anglican ; greater readiness to live with and learn from others, on their terms as well as ours ; less expectation of privilege and status as our due ; and at least a considerable readjustment in the relationship between Church and State in England : these are the minimum requirements of any strategy for the Anglican Communion, at which in nine minutes I have tried to cast a hasty glance. These brief nine minutes of which we have heard so much are an allegory of the time at our disposal to carry them out. Trumpets are sounding ; doors are being opened ; some doors have already been shut. There is not much time left.

Many speakers had suggested that, in view of the ecumenical situation, it was possible that Anglicanism as such had done its work for Christendom and must disappear. Glyn did not think so, as he told the Congress : "If it is God's will it will happen, but I find it hard to believe that God has not still much in his providence for the Anglican Communion to do for a very long time to come." His own unswerving loyalty to Anglicanism, excluding some of the external trappings of the Establishment, had been strengthened by the sight of representatives of Anglicans of seventy-three countries at Toronto ; and he had found it a moving experience to share with so many of his fellow Churchmen in worship and prayer and meeting.

Glyn returned from Toronto in the beginning of September to find that Sheila's life was almost at an end. He had been told in 1958 that she had only five years to live, and during those years the cancer which had invaded her body steadily increased its hold. The doctors had assured him that he could go to Toronto and Sheila had urged him not to stay. But few, if any, knew the extent of her suffering in the last year of her life. Constantly under treatment she was gay and cheerful on her return from hospital; but in the seclusion of her home she had to give way to the exhaustion that she felt. Yet she disguised the seriousness of her illness from her aged mother who died early in September without realising that her daughter was to follow her in a matter of days. To some degree she disguised it even from Glyn himself until he came back from Toronto and she was too weak to keep up the pretence. The strength of will that she had shown in the past was given its final test in this last year of her life and she emerged triumphant. She died 17 September 1963, as greatly mourned in her death as she had been loved in her life. Glyn was one who could not easily give expression to his innermost thoughts. But there is a wealth of feeling and affection in the dedication of the book, *Feeding the Flock*, which he published in 1964. The restraint and economy of the Latin tongue enabled him to express sentiments which would have sounded mawkish in English. It read : *Coniugi amantissimae dilectissimae Resurrectionem gloriosam expectanti.*[19]

Life had to go on. The children were still young and Glyn had to learn to fill the part of both father and mother. His public engagements still beckoned and now there was no Sheila to make sure that he had the peace and quiet to prepare for them. The most immediate task was to prepare for the mission to the University of Durham.

Glyn prepared for Durham with the utmost care. He became concerned because it made such demands on his time, but his friends had little difficulty in convincing him that the work was important. In his last address he summed up what had been attempted :

What has the Mission been all about ? There have been misunderstandings both Christian and non-Christian. So far as the Christians are concerned, it has not been a mission in the sense of trying to convert to any particular brand of Christianity. It has been dealing with Christians of different loyalties and hence has attempted to give broad pictures of the Christian Faith and to show that there is a distinct Christian way of looking at various problems, but that issues confronting us have not in fact got a series of ready-made solutions . . . As far as non-Christians are concerned, many were put off by the word ' mission ' and have stayed away because they feared a kind of revivalist technique. What in fact I have tried to do is to put forward a picture of Christian thinking about half a dozen subjects. It has been a picture drawn not at all by what I understand as an intellectual or a scholar, but by someone,

I hope, reasonably intelligent and well read, with the advantage unlike most of you here, of having had a certain length of years and of life, long enough to have known at first hand something of its joys and sorrows, to have known happiness and sadness, sin and forgiveness.

In the addresses Glyn had grappled with the problems which exercised the minds of young people at this time, race, nuclear weapons, evil and suffering, and he spoke to them with conviction and in a language which they understood. The University's newspaper, the *Palatinate*, declared that the mission had been a great success. It also quoted some reactions : "The first and most obvious was the complete lack of impact upon many ; but the Applebey Theatre was packed to overflowing every night, so that ' many ' cannot have been that many." An atheist questioner at one of the meetings could not see where his views of the world differed from the views put forward by the Bishop, while others declared him to be a Christian agnostic: "This was largely because the Bishop presented his views in such a sane, quiet and reasonable manner . . . but he declared firmly that in the historical figure of Jesus Christ the world has the fullest, most perfect revelation of God that it can receive."

Glyn's influence on young people was now far greater than it ever was before. A number of students then at the Cardiff College of Art remember him for his sympathy and understanding in helping them to found a religious society, called at his suggestion, "The John Marshall Society", in memory of the 15th Century Bishop of Llandaff who had shown some artistic discernment in beautifying his Cathedral. From the majority of his ordinands he received something akin to devotion ; and they learned from their elders, with great surprise, how unpopular Glyn had been at the Church Hostel and at St. Michael's College. He had a great measure of sympathy and open-ness to those ordinands who experienced what he felt were real difficulties, but he could be quite merciless to those whom he thought were running away from their responsibilities or inventing their problems. In these matters he trusted his own judgement implicitly and would hardly listen to any defence. This inflexibility could be a great strength. It was also at times a great weakness in dealing with those who could not or would not do as he wanted.

Inside the diocese Glyn continued the work begun by Archbishop John Morgan of building churches in the vast new housing estates which sprang up in the post-war years. Work was also in progress in the Cathedral. The re-hallowing of the nave of the cathedral had already taken place on 10 April 1957. Then it was possible to proceed with the restoration of the Presbytery and the Lady Chapel. This work was completed by 1960 and the whole of the building was ready for use. The Queen and Prince Philip came to Llandaff on 6 August for the service of thanksgiving for the restoration.

It was now possible to plan a programme of events, ending with a great service on the Cathedral Green on St. Peter's Day 1962 to mark the fourteenth centenary of the diocese. Any doubts about the accuracy of the date were lost in the euphoria of the event. The occasion was also marked by the Bishop's Visitation. In his charge, *Then and Now*, as it was entitled in its printed form, Glyn drew attention to the remarkable similarities which had obtained a hundred years earlier. Then, as now the Cathedral had been restored. In both periods there had been considerable movements of population ; and the general pastoral problems, church accommodation, the shortage of clergy and the use of the Welsh language, were very similar. Then the life of the diocese had been transformed by the growth of industry to which the Church had spoken with an uncertain voice; now there was a similar situation in which Glyn was determined that the Church should learn to speak more clearly.

2. RELATIONS WITH INDUSTRY

In his enthronement address Glyn expressed his pleasure at seeing representative of the Steel Company of Wales, the nationalised industries and the Trade Unions present in the Cathedral.

> These are today vast structures. In such great combinations the vital being at the hearts of them tends to be forgotten, and the human person, the crown of the Creator's work and

The Queen and Prince Philip at Llandaff, 1960

The Bishops of Llandaff and Bangor at Toronto, 1963

Dai Francis and Glyn Simon at the Miners' Home, Bournemouth, 1971

Left to right: Glyn Simon, the Abbot of Caldey, the Archbishop of Cardiff
and the Assistant Bishop of Llandaff at Llys Esgob

the special reflection, however pale, of the Creator himself, is liable to be overlooked . . . It is with persons they must be concerned and somehow their operations must be broken down until, however huge the undertaking, it is at all levels persons who deal with persons ; and men and women who are made in the image of God are not allowed to be "hands" or "units" or "workers" or "block votes". Enormous problems lie ahead . . . Great changes are inevitable, and the Church is in no sense competent to predict them. But she ought to be concerned in them and that immediately. It has recently been pointed out that the men who handle the new powers sincerely desire to know what they ought to do, and that the lines of communication between them and the Church are completely inadequate. Christians are too often ignorant of their skills, or even hostile to their researches. They do not understand our language nor accept our premisses, and we do not understand theirs. Yet it is to the thinkers and technicians who are the driving force of our new revolution that the Church must address herself, and the time is short.

The immediate challenge and opportunity were presented by the Steel Company of Wales at Port Talbot where the establishment of a vast new works had resulted in a concentration of employment involving some 17,000 people. With the help of Father Edward of the Society of St. Francis Glyn began to negotiate for an industrial chaplaincy there ; but patience and persistence were required before the first chaplains started work in August 1960. The approach to the trade union representatives and shop stewards was relatively straightforward. Many of these men had close links with steelworkers in Sheffield where industrial chaplains were known and accepted. Negotiations with the employers were more difficult and it took some time to allay their doubts and suspicions. David Lee, later Rector of Merthyr Tydfil, who was to be the Anglican Chaplain, was sent on an extended training course and the ground was prepared for him in the two Rural Deaneries adjacent to the steel works. Finding a Free Church chaplain was a little more difficult. In the end the Methodist Church came to the rescue and offered to appoint a minister to the Port Talbot circuit who would be enabled to spend most of his time in the steelworks. After three years the Methodists were unable to extend their chaplain's period of office. This was a bitter blow to Glyn, but by this time David Lee's position had become secure and the work was able to go forward without a Free Church Chaplain. David Lee remarks that during the time between his decision to press for an industrial chaplain and the final meeting with the directors in 1959 Glyn had done a great deal of preparation : "He knew a lot about industrial mission and was able to answer the questions and objections from people both in industry and in the Church itself. He confronted his critics, answered their questions, and supported and made possible the work year after year."[20]

Glyn's interest in the chaplaincy was maintained throughout the years that followed. In the beginning David Lee reported to him once a month.

> His knowledge of the work and his understanding of its problems were very deep. On one occasion I mentioned that I was concerned that the discussion groups which I was arranging with men on the shop floors and in some offices did not seem to hold together for more than a few meetings. He at once pointed out to me that this was to be expected, and that it would be a mistake to expect anything like the same continuity in these groups as we took for granted in church services and organisations. The situation was quite different. It was sufficient to convene a group, enable it to meet for a few discussions, and let it break up when it was ready. Relationships with individuals could be maintained, but it would be a mistake to try to keep a group together for the sake of it . . .
> In November 1961 the Bishop visited the steel works and spent a whole day visiting departments. Unlike his previous visits, which had always been conducted by the Managing Director, this time he asked to go with the chaplain and meet some of his informal discussion groups. In these groups he stood up to a barrage of questions about every aspect of the work of the Church, and his own position in national affairs. One group of managers spent nearly an hour with him on the subject of nuclear disarmament. At that time the Bishop was prominent in the Campaign for Nuclear Disarmament and was being criticised for it in many quarters. His meeting head-on with this group of managers in the Central Engineering Shop was typical of his modesty and his firmness in discussion. Whether he convinced them will never be known, but he certainly impressed them, and frequently when I met these men in the works afterwards, they referred with respect to the Bishop and with admiration for the way in which he answered their questions.

Thus far the relationship between Church and industry had proceeded happily. Inevitably a time of testing soon came.

The British Trade Union movement, David Lee remarks, has developed along lines somewhat different from those of the Continent and of the United States. One of the chief differences is that in any large industrial works in Britain, there are to be found many different trade unions rather than just one organisation, as is more probable in other countries. These trade unions fall into two main categories, the process workers' unions and the craft workers' unions. One of the features of British industrial relations has always been the element of conflict between the process and the craft unions. The Steel Company of Wales was no exception to this pattern. The largest and most powerful was the Amalgamated Engineering Union which towards the end of 1963 went on strike and caused the closure of the whole works for seven weeks.

During the 1950s the Company had been in a strong position. It was virtually the only producer of sheet steel and there was a worldwide demand for its product. At that time it had felt bound to maintain production and had conceded very large wage claims to the unions, out of line with national agreements. By 1963 other producers had emerged and there was some competition in the market. The need for some control over wages and for better productivity was being felt by the management. But the A.E.U. felt that it had been left behind and was determined to improve its position in the Abbey Works.

The closure of the works had an immediate and crippling effect upon the whole area. A large number of workers who were ancillary to the steelworks, although not employed by the Company, such as bus drivers, lost their jobs. Many small local shops felt the pinch of a decline in trade and a few actually went out of business. Local communities in industrial South Wales are familiar with industrial disputes and have learnt wisdom. In the first instance, for two or three weeks, it is better to do and say nothing which will aggravate the situation or appear to be interfering. There are always those who try to move into such a situation for selfish reasons, extremist political groups, do-gooders, the insecure and the hysterical. The press is not always helpful, the reporters looking for a story, always pressing men and managers to state opinions and sometimes provoking foolish statements. Industrial workers generally know how to behave in such situations, but while matters during the strike are moving forward secretly, the natural focus of attention is on the fringe and on anyone who is foolish enough to rush in with statements and ill considered solutions.

David Lee was especially careful not to become involved in any public view with the dispute although he knew most of the leading personalities. When the dispute was about three weeks old the Bishop phoned him. Glyn was worried about the strike. He did not want to say the wrong thing, but also he did not want to be accused of not being concerned about it. What then was he to do? David Lee advised caution. The time was not right for a direct approach to either side. He suggested a meeting with the Conciliation Officer of the Ministry of Labour in Cardiff.

The position of Conciliation Officers at that time was that they could talk with both sides in a dispute, carry suggestions between them and propose joint meetings when these might be useful; but they could not take any initiatives of their own such as proposing solutions to problems in industrial relations. Glyn had the feeling, after meeting the Conciliation Officer, that the deadlock might be broken by the intervention of a third party with some practical suggestion. On 13 January 1964 the *Western Mail* published a letter signed by the Bishop of Llandaff, the Archbishop of Cardiff, the Moderator of the Free Church Federal Council and the Chairman of the Cardiff and Swansea District of the Methodist Church, proposing a practical solution to the dispute and calling for concessions on both sides. It had a cool reception from both union and management. But three weeks later the strike was settled. The craftsmen went back to work and a Committee of Inquiry was appointed to look into the whole dispute.

On 5 February the *Western Mail* carried a long centre-page article by the Bishop of Llandaff under the heading: "The strife is o'er but is the battle won?"

This article caused a sensation. Throughout the steelworks men approached me in wonder and astonishment. Seldom had an outsider written such an article about the steelworks in such detail and in such a spirit of bluntness and reasonableness. That it was written by a Church leader caused many to think again about the role of the Church in the world. There were a few who said that the Bishop should confine his ministry to spiritual things, that he ought not to interfere, that he knew nothing of industrial affairs. But the vast majority took a different view. The tone and content of the article helped them to see the dispute in its broader perspective, and to see that a Christian evaluation is relevant.

The article began with an expression of wonder that a dispute so costly in lost wages, production and employment had ended only in an agreement to set up a court of inquiry :

There seems little doubt, from what I can discover, that the prevailing initial reaction in the community at large was one of growing disbelief that in a great industrial undertaking of this sort the two sides should have permitted such a situation to arise. Struggles of this kind, it was felt, should have been as out of date as the Wars of the Roses. Instead, we have had to listen to both sides using language as antiquated as talk in a nuclear age of "drawing the sword" in defence of this or that . . .

Another feature of the dispute which has troubled many people has been the tendency of the contestants to treat the matter as if it was their own private quarrel and to ignore, or even to resent, outside interference. Thus Archbishop Morris' Epiphany appeal to bring in Three Wise Men was treated with silence ; perhaps because of memories of the fiasco of the three wise men of the Cohen Council of 1957, supported by the then Archbishop of Canterbury.

A suggestion by four religious leaders which would not have hindered the solution now arrived at, and would have saved four weeks of unemployment, was dismissed by a Company spokesman with the words : "The Churchmen do not understand the complexities of the situation."

Mr. Wilson's suggestion of a really authoritative court of inquiry has been ignored. Instead, with one change of participant, we have much the same limited group that we have long been familiar with, qualified to conduct a limited inquiry in a situation which is faced with total change of a kind for which a limited inquiry is not qualified. . . .

No one can deny the intricate complexity of the Port Talbot situation, for this stoppage has come at the end, it is said, of 18 months of fruitless argument and is the third in three years. Complex indeed is the jungle of inter-union rivalries which we have been permitted to glimpse ; complex indeed a situation of wage agreements arranged originally on a local basis and now involved in arguments both national and local.

93

Public opinion is not impressed either by the attitude of the craft union to their fellows, or by the company's stand for agreement only on a national basis, when not so long ago, in different and more prosperous times, it rode the wind of its own success and settled everything locally. Now the whirlwind of opposition has overtaken it and an opposite view prevails. It is not easy on the other hand to appreciate the attitude of trade unionists who base their claims on the company's profits in a way which suggests that they have not studied the balance sheets, or else have not believed them.

He went on to plead for the re-establishment of human relationships, for more imagination and for less selfishness, concluding with the words : "The blunt fact remains that in the society of today, which is itself as complex as any part of it, a great undertaking cannot simply be allowed to endanger the community through its own entanglements."

This article earned Glyn an invitation to lunch with the senior management at Port Talbot. The atmosphere at first was chilly, he told David Lee shortly afterwards,

But as the discussion developed it was his long experience in educational work which proved the most important. From his previous discussions and study the Bishop knew that the kind of changes which were needed were not going to be achieved overnight. Something was needed to raise the level of responsibility of working men towards the industry. Since the strike was by craftsmen, it was in this area that he concentrated his attention : "I told them that they ought to scrap the traditional forms of craft apprenticeships and have a more general technical and engineering training which would give more adaptability."

The discussion ended on a friendly note. The Managing Director told Glyn that he did not agree with his article, but he believed him to be sincere in his views. Some years later he wrote to David Lee : "Both my wife and I were tremendous admirers of the late Bishop of Llandaff, Dr. Glyn Simon."

Not long afterwards the steel industry was nationalised and the Abbey Works became part of the British Steel Corporation. At about the same time the Industrial Training Act came into force and gradually transformed the training situation. "It was therefore impossible," David Lee concludes, "for the

Company to do very much about the sort of suggestions which the Bishop had made to them ; but it is not too much to suggest that his ideas might have influenced the thinking of the senior management, most of whom obtained important appointments in the Corporation."

In his Visitation Charge of 1966 Glyn paid tribute to the work done by David Lee at Port Talbot. He also spoke in no uncertain terms about the failure of the Free Churches to maintain a chaplain there :

> The only chaplain there for years has been the Reverend David Lee, supported entirely by this diocese. The promising young Methodist chaplain who started with him was removed after three years, precisely when he was really getting to understand his task, according to the iron rules of the Methodist Connexion. The combined efforts of about a dozen Free Churches have failed to provide for a Free Church chaplain, and the Methodists say they cannot afford one either. So we are left with one man at work amongst fourteen to sixteen thousand men, supported by a voluntary increase in the contributions made by the parishes to central diocesan funds, and the only hope of assistance seems to derive from the same source. This is very discouraging, and one is tempted to wonder whether behind the failure lies the deficient theology of "The Gathered Church".

At first Glyn had encouraged the parish clergy to take an interest in local industry but later he revised this policy. It became clear during the 'sixties that industrial mission was a specialised task which required intensive training for men who could give their whole time to it.

Glyn was much concerned about the mining industry, once predominant in South Wales but now passing through a period of change. He got to know the miners' leaders and paid a number of private and unpublicised visits to their Cardiff offices. He had a good deal to say about coal in his address to the Diocesan Conference in 1959. Then it seemed as though the coal age was coming to an end and the world was in the oil age. He therefore stressed the urgency of long term planning not only on the part of the Coal Board and the Unions but also by the Government.

This diocese owes its present structure very largely to the coal industry, and its future ought to be the concern of every thinking Christian here. Only when Government and officials of one kind and another feel the pressure of a strong and enlightened public opinion will they really work together for the good of all and take measures in time to avert crises which too often find all at a stand . . . The traditional markets and traditional uses of coal seem likely to be on the way out, but that is a very different thing from saying that there is no future for coal. What form that future must take, in the best interest of all, must surely be a major concern of those responsible for the Government of this country whatever its political colour.

He returned to this theme in his Visitation in 1966 when the speed of change seemed to be increasing and there was greater uncertainty about the future. He said that the coal mining industry was a remarkable one, "with a history of cultural and social achievement, marked often by bitterness and suffering, but producing throught it all communities closely knit by a strong sense of comradeship". The published Charge had a significant footnote : "These words were written before the Aberfan Tragedy."

3. ABERFAN

In the morning of 21 October 1966 a small mining village in the diocese of Llandaff became known throughout almost the whole world. It was Aberfan. Standing high on the hill-side above the narrow valley was a huge tip of colliery waste. After some days of heavy rain an avalanche of black slurry engulfed two cottages, a row of terraced houses and the Pantglas Junior School. The death roll was 116 children and 28 adults.

Eryl Thomas, in the Deanery, heard the news flash, and rushed over the Cathedral Green to tell the bishop. Glyn immediately wrote a letter to the *Western Mail*. The Editor was reluctant to publish it, but Glyn insisted and it appeared next morning.

I write with a full heart, which I share with countless thousands, face to face with this terrible tragedy, as I try to prepare myself to go tomorrow to Aberfan to give what help I can to stricken families. Many will feel embittered and enraged at

96

a disaster the causes of which some will ascribe to the ruthless exploitations of the past, others to the procrastination or carelessness of the present. But bitterness will not bring back the dead nor perpetuate their memory. All over South Wales are old tips full of potential danger. The task of removing them or making them safe is vast, far beyond the means of any local authority. I call upon all to support me by every means in their power to have this terrible problem solved at once by the Government which alone has the resources to deal with it. All political and other differences must be put on one side, and surveys made, protective measures taken, and the finance made available now, before greater disasters take place. At any time, and given certain conditions of weather, they may occur, as is well known to everybody who lives in various parts of South Wales. As a first step please write at once in tens of thousands to the Prime Minister, the Minister for Wales and your own Member of Parliament, demanding action now. In this way, though we cannot bring back the dead nor heal the sorrows of the bereaved, we can at least secure that these children shall not have died in vain.

Next morning, 22 October, Glyn was being interviewed by Vincent Kane on the radio programme 'Good morning, Wales'. The transcript of the broadcast conveys the sense of shock felt in the Principality at the magnitude of the disaster, and the questions which arose in people's minds.

Kane : Bishop, a tragedy like this that wipes out little children must be almost inexplicable in Christian terms. People are going to be saying : "How can God allow a thing like this to happen ?"

G.S. : Well of course it is a terrible tragedy. From the Christian point of view the fact that it has happened to little children is, in a way, less dreadful than when it happens to full-grown men and women because these children were particularly prepared ; they'd only just said their prayers and for Christians this was the movement from one room of their Father's house to another much nearer to him. It does not make it any easier for parents at the moment. Later I hope they will come to see that. But, of course, this is not like an earthquake or some kind of terrific natural disaster. Before we blame God for this. we must be quite sure that men to whom he has given reason and conscience had done in the past and have done recently all that they ought to have done to

97

prevent this from happening. Blaming God is sometimes a way of getting out of finding out what really the causes of the disaster are ; and the main hope is that the causes of this disaster will be urgently and independently sought for, as the Prime Minster has promised. But I can see myself how difficult these things make it for people to believe in God. I find— I don't pretend otherwise—I often find it very difficult to believe in God ; but I find any other way of looking at the world and the frightful things that happen in it very much more difficult.

Kane : What consolation can you offer as a church leader to those people who have lost children or lost parents, the people who have been bereaved generally ?

G.S. : I can't really say until I see them because each circumstance is different. I can at least offer them the consolation of somebody who has lost a baby of his own and has lost his wife, and this makes a commonwealth of suffering which sometimes helps. But, of course, the real work of consolation will be done by the ministers and clergy who are on the spot, who are very often forgotten, who know their people very much better than I.

Kane : You are not just a spiritual leader, Bishop. In a way you are a social leader in this part of the world as well. How do you feel in that capacity ?

G.S. : Well, I feel angry, as I often feel where the miners are concerned, because this is part of the terrible price that is quite happily and unconsciously accepted by the community, and I very much hope that this may mean an urgent and serious look, and action taken on the highest level about other tips which all of us know exist potentially dangerous up and down South Wales. If this happens, then this tragedy won't have been entirely a pointless one.

Kane : Do you think that we ought almost to start a crusade to have all these other tips made safe ?

G.S. : Well I think so. I see no other hope at all. I can't do anything much by myself. I hope there will be a wave of popular pressure which will force action. It is nonsense to say that money is'nt available, but it's got to be available on a big scale that only a Government can find.

Kane : I believe that immediately now you are going straight to Aberfan. What do you hope to do there ?

G.S. : I don't really know until I get there. I do know that I am going to see the parents or relatives of the teachers

98

who have been lost, because in our natural anxiety about the children we have sometimes forgotten the awful sorrow of the parents of those who have been teaching. I hope to go and see fifteen to twenty children themselves in Merthyr Hospital, to see the Mayor of Merthyr, and take such other chances as may come my way, which may be very few because of the conditions.[21]

The next day was Sunday and Glyn broadcast in the evening on television. He spoke quietly and briefly, bringing to the people of Aberfan the love and sympaty of the many thousands of people on whose behalf he spoke : "If I had not known for myself, sorrow over the death of someone I loved and love still, I would not have dared to speak tonight . . . I would like to share with you some words of Scripture from Isaiah that have often helped me much : ' Fear not . . . I have called you by name, you are mine. When you pass through the waters I will be with you ; and through the rivers, they shall not overwhelm you.' "

The Welsh Members of Parliament did not like the forthright stand that Glyn had taken. They held a special meeting at the House of Commons 26 October when it was reported that they were angry at the advice given by the Bishop ; and the Minister for Welsh Affairs wrote rather petulantly to the *Western Mail* to say that the Welsh Office had better things to do than to receive large numbers of letters of protest. But Glyn had merely done what he thought a bishop ought to do in the exercise of that pastoral ministry which belonged both to him and to the Vicar of Merthyr Vale, the parish in which Aberfan is situated ; and few bishops, if any, have been called upon to face pastoral problems of the magnitude presented by the tragedy at Aberfan. Accompanied by the incumbent, Thomas Wilfred Jones, Glyn visited all the bereaved families in the area. His pastoral concern for them was much appreciated at the time and has long been remembered. When he spoke at this time, he was speaking not only for the diocese of Llandaff but for the whole of Wales.

Glyn was appointed to the committee which administered the Aberfan Disaster Fund. Considerable sums of money passed through Llys Esgob for the Bishop of Llandaff had become a focal point in the eyes of many both at home and abroad. These donations were carefully listed and despatched, in the main to the Mayor of Merthyr Tydfil, but in a few instances, and according to the wishes of the donors, to specific objects in Aberfan.

In 1969 it was necessary to appoint a new incumbent and Glyn chose a young man whom he had know in Swansea and Brecon, Michael Short. The new vicar was tempted to begin his incumbency in a blaze of publicity, for not a fewre presentatives of the news media asked him for his reactions to his appointment. He blandly replied that he considered it to be a normal parochial appointment, and no different from a nomination to any other parish. But Michael knew that he had Glyn's full support in the task which he undertook and which was not without its problems. Firstly he had to set about building a new church. The former church, built in 1926, had long been affected by the subsidence of the ground on which it stood. The heavy traffic which passed by after the disaster completed the process and rendered it unsafe. A public appeal was launched and Glyn had the pleasure of consecrating the new church 31 October 1970. The earlier church had been dedicated to Our Lady. The new church was dedicated to St. Mary and the Holy Innocents. Glyn and his family came back next day for the celebration of the first Eucharist in the church which now stood as a memorial to the victims of the tragedy, and as a symbol of new life in the community which he had taken to his heart.

7

TIMES OF CHANGE

1. CONTEMPORARY PROBLEMS

The vocation of the Church, Glyn declared, was to be as leaven in the mass of society. It was to be "a disturbing and invigorating influence" ; and these words can aptly be applied to him. Yet he was critical of those Christians who seemed to be preoccupied with economic and political problems :

> The goals of much twentieth century religion seems to be (a) social amelioration (b) political and economic reform (c) earthly and temporal welfare . . . and they are all of this world. There is of course a very real sense in which all this kind of activity is the concern of religion . . . But "our citizenship is in heaven". We must not identify Christianity with enthusiasm for social justice and reform,. To do so is to make religion barely distinguishable from secular humanitarianism.

The word is "involvement", he remarked, "and a very suitable word it is provided we are clear about its dangers". He himself was always conscious that as a bishop it was his duty to defend the Christian Faith ; and he never lost sight of the timeless and supernatural character of the Faith which, he would admit, from time to time required reinterpretation, but which, he would insist, could not be changed. Given this proviso he was prepared to be a single-minded adherent of those causes to which he gave his support. On many social matters he could be as modern and progressive as some of those with whom he rubbed shoulders at this time. But there was a limit.

His own "involvement" and concern for social amelioration were considerable. His sermon before the British Association which met in Cardiff in 1960 gave him the opportunity to expound his views on subjects which a decade later were to assume an ominous importance.

> Bad farming, bad husbandry, bad forestry, the reckless expenditure of minerals or of oil, these too are morally wrong for they are the wrong response to the environment in which God

has set us. When religion and husbandry and agriculture and forestry are joined together, then we get not only growing understanding of life and reverence for the earth, the good earth, but also an enthusiasm for new inventions and new techniques, which apart from this union are often resisted, as well as a deepening understanding of our religion and its significance for daily life.

But ecology was then a word which was not as widely known as it is now. The population problem was then under discussion and not a few thought it could be solved by contraception. Glyn took the discussion to a deeper level :

> There is no moral justification for maintaining the standard of living to which we and our friends have become accustomed while two-thirds of the world are below subsistence level . . . When food and materials are squandered and wasted on a dreadful scale in our own and other lands, in such a situation we are face to face with what is morally evil and wrong, with sin against our neighbour, against ourselves, against posterity against the Natural Order, against God himself.

These words, too, have taken on a deeper significance with the passing years.

He was well to the fore in the controversy over nuclear weapons which in those days generated a good deal of heat. His diary for 1959 contains a number of entries relating to the Campaign for Nuclear Disarmament. He spoke, for example, at the European Congress held in London 17 January, at public meetings at Oxford and Hereford and at students' meetings at Cardiff and Swansea ; and he gained himself such headlines in the Press as "Bishop hits out at Church split over H bomb". The Welsh Bench itself was divided on this issue, for Archbishop Morris took the view that nuclear weapons, terrible though they were, were essential deterrents to war in the the world today. A host of young people wrote to Glyn at this time, most of them saying that they did not go to Church but they would like to come to hear him preach, while assuring him of their admiration for the stand he had taken. To one who wrote to thank him for an article he had written in the *Church of England Newspaper* he replied :

I admit to no optimism. No responsible government could unilaterally surrender the use of nuclear weapons without a mandate from those to whom it is responsible. Of that there is no sign at all ; it calls for a degree of self-sacrifice quite beyond the grasp of a civilisation firmly based, however "Christian" the West may call istself, on a secular materialism. But that does not excuse us from persisting in our attempts to change public opinion, and in witnessing against evil on moral grounds.

In his Durham addresses he had hard things to say about the division of opinion in the Church :

It seems impossible to think that a Church founded upon the Lord Jesus Christ can ever sanction or support the use of nuclear weapons. But the Church is not sufficiently converted, and insufficiently "not of this world" ; it is not in a position to suggest on a basis of political responsibility the renunciation of the use of the H-bomb. Possibly here, more than anywhere else, lies its condemnation. It has so long compromised with Caesar that it cannot get away from him. It has so long accepted the evils of war that, when they come at last to their logical and horrible conclusion it can only speak with a divided voice. Hence the matter becomes one for the individual Christian conscience.

Formerly Glyn had accepted the concept of the "just war" and regarded the war against Hitler as one in which the country was justifiably engaged : "But as it went on with its deliberate attacks by both sides on the civilian population, its area bombing, its growing destruction of the fruits of civilisation, both spiritual and moral, doubts multiplied on the part of increasing numbers of people about its justice and the traditional sense of the word in this context." Then came the new bomb which changed the situation entirely. He had no patience with the argument that the difference was only quantitative : "So vastly greater is the quantitative effect that the weapon is qualitatively different." Nor was he moved by the argument often used at the time, "Better dead than Red".

These principles were applied to Vietnam where, as he saw it, "a peaceful and gentle population has been subjected for a quarter of a century to the terrible results of a merciless ideological struggle". His conlusions were expressed in a letter to the *Times* in 1965 :

I have been hoping to read in your columns statements by Christian leaders about American policy in Vietnam. I am sure that I speak for very many Christians who are horrified by the use there of napalm bombs and gas. The minimising phrases put out to describe the gases used must not blind us to the fact that in defiance of the Geneva Protocol of 1925 this is an opening of the doors to chemical warfare. Napalm bombs in Korea roasted whole villages and left people alive, blind and skinless. These are horrific and inexcusable weapons to use. But the really terrifying factor in the situation is that the war in Vietnam is part of a world-wide war for the minds and souls of men, and that America seems to believe that this war can be won by military might and by displays of ferocious power. The Chinese leaders are convinced that Communism hold the secret of human happiness and passionately believe in it. Christians believe that this secret lies with Christ and his Gospel, and that his message is one of love and peace. It seem; unlikely that this will be very clearly seen amongst clouds of gas and the flames of jellied petrol dispensed, as the victims will believe, by a Christian nation.

Were Mr. Wilson in Opposition his protests would be loud and clear. Now that he is in power he faces an Opposition not likely to disturb him on this issue. It is left to individuals, convinced in conscience of the iniquity and futility of the present American policy, to condemn it as clearly and publicly as they can.

He had already concluded that, even without nuclear weapons, the conditions for a "just war" were no longer relevant under modern circumstances. With the press and radio controlled in wartime, and in some countries more or less perpetually controlled it was no longer possible for a nation to assess the justice of its cause.

Some of his associates in the Campaign for Nuclear Disarmament thought they saw in Glyn a modern and progressive bishop. It was at their suggestion that the solicitors who were acting for the publishers of the book, *Lady Chatterley's Lover*, approached him as an expert who might be prepared to give evidence in support of their clients. They had not recognised the rigorist who read the copy of the book which was sent to him, and who returned it with the comment that publication would not be for the public good and he could not support it. He went on to give cogent reasons :

104

Lawrence's aim of getting rid of "the dirty little secret" attitude to sex is today beside the point . . . Making even the widest allowance, some at least of the unexpurgated scenes seem to me pornographic. The general merits, literary and otherwise, of the expurgated passages are, in my judgement, insufficient to outweigh these other considerations. The book's literary merits as a whole do not seem to me to place it among Lawrence's better work .

When the Archbishop of Canterbury came out firmly against the publication of the book, Glyn wrote to thank him for his stand and sent him a copy of his letter to the publisher's solicitors. Archbishop Fisher replied :

Thank you for your letter about the recent book trial. I am very glad to know that you were approached to give evidence, and that you stoutly refused. What you said in your letter in answer to the invitation was very good indeed.

The Archbishop went on to say that the ecclesiastical experts who gave evidence at the trial thought that they must speak with the voice of prophecy ; but he doubted if the courtroom was a suitable place for a prophet.

The problem of race-relationships became more acute at this time. Glyn remarked at Durham that it was "one of the great unsolved problems of our time which provides a special illustration of the Christian view of man". It was not a monopoly of the white races though history had cast them in a leading role for it. There were encouraging features in the depressing picture. Children left to themselves, whether black or white, soon overcame the intitial fear of something different and strange ; while the presence in all parts of the world of a numerous half-caste population showed that there was no inbred racial antipathy between the sexes. Colour prejudice was of no great antiquity ; it had come about as a result of moral, political and economic problems, "the same causes in fact which give rise to hostility and bitterness within a sane community".

Only a firm belief in the value of the individual in God's sight can secure the right of every man to be treated as a man . . . which will save us from self-consciousness in our attitude towards them which is even more hated than frank hostility. The right attitude of mind is only possible if we see ourselves constantly in Christ, at the feet of God, and realise our common brotherhood together. It is on grounds of this kind that Christians feel bound to condemn racial policies . . . wrong because they are based, in the last resort on the denial of the dignity of man as the child of God.

In this matter Glyn certainly practised what he preached. He was loud in his protests in 1966 against the Government of Rhodesia and its supporters in this country. "What is involved," he declared, "is the nature of man and the rights of each individual, whatever his race and colour . . . This ought to be, above all questions of kith and kin and so forth, the proper and urgent moral concern of every Christian in this situation."

Protests against the policy of apartheid in South Africa found a rallying point in 1970 in the mounting oppostion to the proposed tour of the South African Cricket Team, and Glyn was well to the fore. "We must do all that we can to protest," he wrote. "For my own part, if the Glamorgan Cricket Club goes on with its fixture with South Africa next year, I shall give up my membership of it and I hope many others will do the same in view of the grave principles involved." When the Tour was cancelled the Press Association asked him for a statement and he said :

One is naturally sympathetic with the many people who were looking forward to seeing in action probably the best cricket XI in the world today. But the strain the Tour would have imposed on an already tense racial situation, the possibility of violence and the ruin facing the Edinburgh Games makes one thankful that it has been called off. Nor must we forget the Police whose calmness and courage in dealing with demonstrators of one kind or another will not now be called upon for this particular situation.

On both these occasions Glyn received a large number of letters. To his dismay, most of them were highly vituperative, and these he bundled up and sent to the National Library of Wales so that future generations might have some idea of the strong feelings aroused by the racial problems of the 1960s. He was pleased to note that most of these letters came from England. Very few came from Wales. This seemed to confirm his opinion that race relations in the Prinicpality were a good deal better than they were in other parts of the United Kingdom.

The Diocesan Leaflet provided Glyn with a convenient platform from which to comment on the life of the times. In 1965 he looked out on the social scene of his diocese and saw much that made him fear for the future :

> I greatly enjoyed the classical education I received, and not least the study of the history of Greece and Rome. But I sometimes find it depressing to look back on, in the kind of times we are living in. So many of the characteristics which marked the decline of those civilisations are to be seen today that it is difficult to be optimistic about what lies ahead of us. There is the breakdown in religion, the increase in violence, economic crises, a decline in moral standards, an abnormal interest in sex, the rise of new nations on the borders of former empires, the growing approximation of professional sport to the standards of gladiatorial shows, to mention only a few. But more disturbing than anything else is the sense of a loss of nerve, and a general feverish pursuit of enjoyment of every kind.

He went on to refer to the status symbols of the newly affluent South Wales, which apparently included "champagne at parties instead of sherry : mink coats instead of musquash", not to mention the numerous clubs and casinos which had appeared.

Letters came back to Llys Esgob from all parts of the world, including a press cutting from a German newspaper ; but in the next issue of the Leaflet Glyn sadly concluded : "Mink and champagne seem news, while clubs and casinos are not ; what I said about the first was reported ; what I said about the second was not." He had no objections to clubs, but, as they spent such vast sums on their improvement, he thought it would be nice to hear of some spontaneous gift, for Feed the Hungry, by way of example.

On the approach of the General Election of 1970 Glyn had something to say about the housing situation.

> One would certainly like to see fewer offices (on which financial returns are so swift and considerable) with their tendency to turn the hearts of our towns into concrete deserts. One would wish, too, to see greater flexibility on the matter of improvement

107

and adaptation grants for older houses . . . Large grants for the alteration of these seem at first sight costly, but what is this in comparison with the cost of the little horseboxes which sprawl across so many areas . . . There is scope here for an imaginative Minister of Housing, but perhpas this phrase is a contradiction in terms.

The *News of the World* got hold of the leaflet and sent a reporter to Llys Esgob. The result was that Glyn appeared on the front page of the paper in full episcopal attire (and, as he put it, "underneath a large blonde") with a long account of what he had written alongside.

What he had said was perfectly right, and now local authorities are adapting older houses just as he said they should. But a former Minister of Housing saw the newspaper report and wrote to point out that the matter was not quite as simple as Glyn seemed to think. Lord Greenwood wrote :

I cannot believe that you are suggesting that the central government should have greater powers than they have at present to interfere with local democracy. I can just imagine a future diocesan leaflet pleading for greater decentralisation and for local democracy, possibly even quoting William Temple's views on democracy . . . But most surprising is your reference to the need for "an imaginative Minister of Housing". This seems to be gratuitously uncharitable, particularly from the Archbishop of a Principality in which the Minister of Housing's powers are almost entirely vestigial, and where practically all the powers I had in England were vested in the Secretary of State (for whom I had always understood you shared my own deep affection and great respect).

The letter came as an unwelcome surprise. Glyn was, as he remarked to George Thomas, the former Secretary of State for Wales, "sorry to have upset so nice a person as Tony Greenwood". Though gently worded, the letter implied that Glyn did not know what he was talking about and that he had been uncharitable. He therefore tried to clarify his position.

I am sorry if my views grieved you. I had no particular Minister in mind when I wrote, as this painful housing problem does not seem to alter much under any government. I am sorry you should think that I wrote unthinkingly ; believe me, I know too much about the evils and sufferings of the housing situation to write lightly about it.

What he wanted was to see housing become an absolute government priority : "I am not party-minded in this matter and I think Macmillan came nearest to the kind of thing I have in mind ; he managed to make the Ministry of Housing exciting, and relatively practical results followed."

This was not exactly an eirenicon. A lengthy correspondence followed in which Lord Greenwood bore down upon him with all the facts and figures at his command. Glyn resisted stoutly to the end but he was fighting a losing battle. It was, however, a private correspondence. Lord Greenwood sought no publicity for his views.

Archbishop Anthony Bloom published an article on Christians in Russia in the *Church Times* in September 1970. Glyn's attention was caught by the statement that the Soviet leaders on the whole discounted any specific Church or Christian intervention, but actually paid considerable attention to protests on a Government level. He immediately wrote to the Prime Minister quoting what Bloom had written and adding: "I write in the hope that you may feel it right and proper to make some representations in the right quarter on behalf of large numbers of our fellow-Christians whose lot is never bright and sometimes is very hard indeed." The Prime Minister, Mr. Edward Heath, replied that the report in the *Church Times* was correct, and it was the reflection of the increased volume of news about the fate of Russian Christians which was now reaching the West. It was difficult to make direct representations to a Government about their own nationals, but, Mr. Heath wrote : "The Government should take a firm line. I would agree with Archbishop Bloom's view that the Soviet Union is not insensitive to international opinion and we shall do what we can." Glyn was delighted with this response because, he wrote in reply : "It will enable me to give a discreet answer to those who criticise me for attacking South Africa and Apartheid and saying nothing about Christians in Russia. You may be absolutely confident that my note will be framed in such a way as not to involve in any way any suggestion that I have been in touch with you."[22]

The winds of theological change hardly disturbed him. In his Charge of 1966 he dismissed the New Theology with the words : "It will pass, and leave behind it whatever in it is of permanent value for our better understanding and use of the riches of the Gospel." Two years later, in his lecture at Canterbury, he spoke of theologians who wrote wildly, even irresponsibly :

> It is one thing to say that we must be prepared in each generation, and never more so than in ours, for a reforming and explaining of the Faith. It is quite another thing to do this in such a way that nothing will remain of the original shape, or to argue that the new forms must be entirely contemporary. To exalt the contemporary into an abolute in its own right is a dangerous thing to do. But those who try to do this reforming and reshaping have made us realise that there are problems and that the problems are not as simple as they seem.

There he urged that the reverent agnosticism with which many a great thinker or scientist contemplates the results of his own thinking or discoveries is very fitting for the Christian apologist in times when all is on the move. "They should note the reserve of the great Catholic Creeds, the absence of clear-cut theories about God's final purposes which we find there."

Yet he could show alarm at some of the consequences of this theological ferment. About this time a new member of staff was appointed to St. Michael's College, one who came from a decidedly evangelical background. Glyn feared for the Tractarian tradition of St. Michael's though he knew quite well that this tradition generally was being considerably modified. He was not reassured by a brief conversation with the Warden, Chancellor O. G. Rees, so he wrote him a letter which reveals his determined resistance to some aspects of theological change.

> What I have to say will run the risk of being dismissed out of hand as "out of touch" or even "clerical", a word now much used perjoratively by those who feel that they are men of our times, competent to rewrite in terms of a decade not merely a thousand years of theology but the whole of biblical beliefs as well . . . More serious, however, are the traditions of St. Michael's College, the aims with which it was founded and the convictions which ;inspired |the |notable generosity through which it still survives. I knew both Archbishop Green and Mr. Wilfred de Winton personally, and why they prayed and worked so hard and raised so much money for a Welsh theological

college. It does not seem to be right or even ethical or even Christian to treat such conviction and generosity lightly. No doubt many of the practices and even particular beliefs held by these men are now outmoded. But a permanent truth remains. There are, I suppose, two main interpretations of Christianity, Catholic and Protestant ; the first might be described, broadly speaking, as Incarnational, the second as centring on the Atonement. I have no doubt myself as to which is the true one, or the wider and richer, or that it includes the second ; while the second often tends to minimize the first. From the first Catholic interpretation follow, as you will know, certain doctrines of the Church, the Ministry, and the Sacraments—to which the second sits lightly. The beliefs, the hopes, the plans and the generosity of the founders and benefactors of St. Michael's College were the result of deep conviction as to the truth of the Catholic view of the Work of Christ, the Church, the Ministry and the Sacraments. If I understood you rightly the other day (and our conversation was admittedly hurried and scrappy), you were inclined to regard all this as out of date, "clerical", and to regard all these profound differences about the Christian faith as "the product of the vicarage". Nevertheless I hope you will agree with me that we must not as Christians treat lightly what has been handed down to us, nor set aside as irrelevant the aims and hopes of those who set St. Michael's College on its way. True we cannot opt out of the modern world or take an attitude of implacable conservatism. There must always be change, but not of such a kind as to involve a digging up of the foundations on which our founders and benefactors built so wisely and so well. I hope you will forgive the inordinate length of this letter. It is written out of deep concern and conviction, and in no spirit of carping criticism.

The Warden thought that he was being attacked and his own words misinterpreted. He therefore offered to answer any questions put to him in writing, even though, he remarked : "Such a proceeding would be reminiscent of the altercation between Bishop Philpotts and Gorham. I would certainly not wish to be regarded as a 20th Century Gorham and I doubt whether your Lordship would wish to be compared with Philpotts."

Glyn's reply revealed some irritation :

I am sorry that you seem to have taken my letter so amiss. You seem to have misunderstood its purport for you speak of "having to safeguard your position in the strongest possible terms". So far as I know, no-one is attacking it ; certainly not I, for if I had been I should have gone about things in a very different way. I certainly do not wish to cast you in the role of a Gorham, a role wholly unsuitable to you.

But by this time he had developed a patience and a capacity for listening which had not been apparent in the earlier stages of his career, and so he concluded : "I would welcome a full discussion with you on matters which deeply concern me, and I can assure you that if you do come, as I hope you will, it will be nothing more than that."

2. THE ECUMENICAL SEA

In the early 1960s ecumenical hopes ran high. The bishops had come back from the Lambeth Conference of 1958 duly conscious of their responsibility to further the cause of Church Unity. The important Faith and Order Conferences at Lund and Montreal, and the meeting of the World Council of Churches in New Delhi in 1961 seemed to have set the ecumenical movement on a sure foundation ; and in 1964 the first British Conference on Faith and Order held at Nottingham called upon the member churches "To covenant together to work and pray for the inauguration of union by a date agreed amongst them". In the enthusiasm of the moment it was hoped that the date would be no later than Easter Day 1980.

The Anglican Congress at Toronto in 1963 took due note of this new impetus towards Christian unity. Glyn wrote :

Although there may not be many specific references to them in the Official Report and speeches of the Congress, everyone was much aware of our separated brethren, Christians of other loyalties than ours . . . Many people were conscious of the urgent problem of Christian disunity as it confronts the Church in many parts of the world. It was plain that in several places local schemes of union will be proceded with, and that this would mean that Anglican dioceses would be found in future as parts of the Church of such and such a country, and no longer, strictly speaking, a part of the Anglican Communion. In this connection there was a fair amount of use of some such phrase as, "It is the vocation of the Anglican Church to disappear". It was plain that this was a phrase which did not by any means generally commend itself. The Anglican Communion, if it is anything, is not a Protestant denomination, but consciously and from the beginning a part of the One Holy Catholic and Apostolic Church with the Creeds, the Ministry and the Sacraments of the one Church. The only sense in which it can disappear, unless the wisdom of God should otherwise order it, is by its absorption into the unity of this One Church.

This was his ideal for unity. It was not something which could be hastily accomplished, for, as he remarked in an address at Birmingham in 1962 : "Fundamental truths of the Faith must not be abandoned in a moment of fear or in impatience with delay, or in the desire to get quick results." On that occasion he seemed to favour the South India method because it was prepared to move slowly "in an endavour to find out in what ways the Holy Spirit is leading", in contrast to other schemes which seemed to be rooted in ambiguity. But this does not mean that he gave it his unqualified approval. He became increasingly suspicious of the way in which the ecumenists of the time seemed to be moving, towards the creation of a kind of super-Church. Speaking at Pusey House, Oxford, in 1964, he made his doubts very plain.

I am not at all sure that I ought to have said "yes" to your Principal's suggestion that I should preach on "The Recovery of Unity". I am simply a busy diocesan bishop whose voyages on that great waterway, comparatively recently discovered, the Ecumenical Sea, are very limited. Mine has been the part of the watcher on the sea-shore, gazing with wonder at the busy traffic passing by. There go the ships, of various lines, some very imposing. Who could fail to miss the great boats of the W.C.C. line, constantly on the move, touching at almost every port, however remote, and hardly for a moment at harbour ? There are the lesser boats of the B.C.C., and even smaller lines fussing and puffing about on shorter voyages round the coasts of Wales and Ireland. The cargo they seek is one and the same —unity—but in their search they seem sometimes to come back with other cargoes which betoken lack of space for the real thing when they have at last discovered it. Very large packing cases have abounded, labelled with strange names, C.B.M.S. I.M.C. ; in a very early voyage there was a mysterious package called U.N.W.R.A.P.N.E. which, I suspect, came in by mistake and whose contents have never been discovered. Let us hope there is no significance in the fact that several of the parcels do not appear to be very clearly labelled, so that the Anglican lines have read M.R.A. for M.R.I. ; and M.E.C.C.A. has suggested that the quest for unity has gone even further than had been realised.[23]

I hope I have not sounded too flippant, yet underneath the flippancy lies a doubt as to where all these activities are leading. If, for example, some form of visible unity in the non-Roman world were to come about, is there not a real danger of over powering centralisation in a vast and expensive H.Q. with more and more people taken from pastoral and teaching and even writing work to tasks of administration ? It would be a tragedy if the recovery of unity were to be accompanied by a vast super-organisation. There is no reason to suppose that a Pan-Protestant bureaucracy would be any less vulnerable to temptation than a Roman Curia. As we move forward towards the recovery of unity, we need to keep a very sharp eye on the administrative growth of the B.C.C. and the W.C.C. and all the rest of them. There go the ships, if I may return to my nautical metaphor; do not let us forget that the Psalmist added : "and there is that Leviathan".

He went on to argue that unity must be found in diversity ; but he also said that the search for unity is like the search for the Kingdom of God on earth : "It is an ideal to which we must always strive : the ideal may, perhaps must, never be realised, but we are never excused from its pursuit." He also firmly stated that the idea of a great non-Roman, even a non-Orthodox, Church made little appeal to him. It was therefore to be expected that he would venture out on the Ecumenical Sea only with the utmost caution.

In 1969 a motion before the Governing Body requested the Bench of Bishops "to introduce a bill to enable approval to be given on behalf of the Church in Wales to the inauguration of Stage I of the Anglican-Methodist Proposals". Glyn had already made know his opposition to the scheme. He disliked its complexities, "its many ambiguities, its resolute decision to sweep under the carpet numbers of quite unresolved difficulties, all potential sources of strife and bitterness" and so could not support it ; and he wrote : "I hope to promote in the Governing Body and elsewhere suggestions for a more realistic and less tortuous approach to the great and longed-for end." The motion was passed by a large majority, but as the Anglican-

Methodist Scheme failed to get the required majority in England, there was no point in pursuing the matter in Wales.

After the meeting between the Archbishop of Canterbury with Pope Paul in 1966 it was agreed to set up a Joint Preparatory Commission which Glyn was invited to join. He attended the Conference at Gazzada in January 1967, finding himself in congenial company and "keenly aware of the pain of the wounds of the Church of Christ, his Mystical Body, which must be probed deeply if they are to be truly healed".

A sermon preached at the Anglican-Orthodox Festival in London 11 October 1969 reveals Glyn's thoughts on another branch of Christendom. The story of Anglican-Orthodox relationships, so far as negotiations and prayers were concerned, had lasted over one hundred years "which make the Anglican-Methodist negotiations or even the South India situation seem positively hasty . . . but one does feel that in a sense an invisible power rose up between them like a spectre and beckoned them apart". On the Orthodox side the spectre was the need for complete and genuine unity of doctrine and the requirement for a decision by the whole Orthodox Church ; on the Anglican side there was another spectre "which can be identified as Anglican comprehensiveness, a phenomenon, as more than one Orthodox statement has made clear, unintelligible to Orthodox theologians ; and small wonder for it sometimes baffles us who have lived with it for three or four centuries." This comprehensiveness, however, had to be seen as something deliberately and consciously accepted :

To be an Anglican means to belong to a communion which for the best part of four hundred years has contrived to make workable a form of Christian union which others are still talking about. This is no accident ; it has come about as the result of deliberate policy adopted from the first . . . The result has been that there have been held together over the centuries very various types of Christians who have been enabled to receive Communion in the same Church and to remain in unity with one another. It is a Church best to be understood not in terms of either of its extreme wings, or in terms of the "outspoken clerics" who from time to time arise and are by the Press or the B.B.C. "accounted to be pillars" ; but in terms of the mass of middle-of-the-road men. These are the typical English churchmen who have a sense of the continuity of the Church of God, who like to have divine worship conducted with decency and with dignity, who believe in the necessity of an ordered Liturgy and an ordered Ministry. They have never cared much for Theology and distrust over-precise definitions, fearing their divisive effects . . . Individually such men may hold, for example, a receptionsit doctrine of the Holy Communion, or a high doctrine of the Real Presence in the Sacrament. They may, and probably do, think those who differ from them mistaken, but they know that the Prayer Book will not allow them to unchurch them.

But the sermon was no mere apology for Anglicanism. Glyn repeated some scathing remarks he had made in *The Landmark* about the typical churchman of the Establishment ; and in the first draft of his sermon he was very critical of the Provinces of Canterbury and York for sometimes acting as though they *were* the Anglican Communion. Such a Church needed very much the strength of faith and order and worship which Orthodoxy could bring. It needed Orthodox spirituality and prayer "if we are to move beyond the rather unsupernatural and unsacramental outlook and practice of the average Church of England layman". Orthodoxy could also receive much from Anglicanism ; but meanwhile he offered to this suffering Church, whose steadfastness could be seen in its roll of modern martyrs, his admiration and his hope that the mutual contacts might steadily develop until they could speak to the world as One Church of the Living God.

Resolution 45 of the Lambeth Conference of 1968 recommended "that in order to meet special pastoral needs of God's people, under the direction of the bishop, Christians duly baptised in the name of the Holy Trinity and qualified to receive Holy Communion in their own Churches may be welcomed at the Holy Table in the Anglican Communion". This was probably in Glyn's mind when he declared his intention of promoting "suggestions for a more realistic approach" to Church Unity than those presented by the Anglican-Methodist negotiations. In 1969 he, as Archbishop and on behalf of the Bench of Bishops, presented to the Governing Body a proposal for limited intercommunion. The preamble read : "That the Governing Body, giving thanks for the increasing recognition by all Churches of God's gift of unity in Christ and of the need to manifest this unity in the world, supports the following statement of the Bench of Bishops." The statement was a long one but it resolved a number of problems which for historical reasons had been more acute in Wales than elsewhere. It enabled incumbents to invite Nonconformist ministers "to offer prayer or to preach at services of the Church in Wales, other than at the Holy Eucharist, that are intended to promote the unity of Christians and the mission of God in the world". It also stated that, subject to the oversight of the diocesan bishop, "baptised communicant members of a Trinitarian Church may be admitted to Holy Communion in the Church in Wales in such conditions as follows". The conditions laid down were spelled out in greater detail in the dioceses. Despite his occasional flippancy, and though he was more at home in conversations with Roman Catholics and Orthodox than with Nonconformists, this motion is sufficient indication that Glyn was in earnest on the subject of Church Unity.

3. THE CHURCH'S ORGANISATION

The Second General Visitation of the diocese of Llandaff, undertaken in 1966, had in its published form the bold title, *A Time of Change*. It also contained the charges given at the Primary Visitation of Llandaff Cathedral. Since his days at the Llandaff Deanery Glyn had revised his ideas about cathedrals and he expressed his opinions at his Diocesan Conference in 1959 : "I sometimes wonder how we would have been placed today if twelve dioceses had been made in Wales . . . if Deans and Chapters had been abolished and the Bishops had returned to the proper use of the Cathedrals as their own churches in which they were surrounded by their own officers." He returned to this theme in his Visitation, especially since the report of the Cathedrals Commission of the Governing Body had just been published.

A canonry ought to be regarded as an office and not an honour. Ideally it is an office that should be filled by archdeacons and other clergymen engaged with the bishop in diocesan work and held only for a number of years . . . It seems to me from the point of view of Cathedral and Diocese a matter of regret that the Report contented itself simply with abolishing the present canonical system and did not go on to propose that its place should be taken by rural deans. This had been urged in more than one quarter, and certainly in this diocese the rural deans, with the archdeacons, are the nearest approach I have to a bishop's council, and I meet them regularly.

He looked back, rather with regret, to the factors which "combined to break up the old pattern of the cathedral as the headquarters of the bishop with his staff around him, led by him in conference and prayer in the church that was especially his" ; and he elaborated on the price paid by Chapters "for setting themselves up as little ecclesiastical republics" who sometimes resented the presence of the bishop in his own church, so that peace loving bishops kept as much away from their cathedrals as they could. But this yearning for an idealized past did not blind him to the realities of the present, and he could not but glory in Llandaff Cathedral as it then was. It was, he said, passing through probably one of its most active and successful periods ; and he paid tribute to the "energy, organizing power and musical and other gifts" of the then Dean, Eryl Thomas. Yet the general drift of the Charge may have reminded the Dean and Chapter of some slight tension between them and their bishop some years before. There is little doubt that formerly Glyn had been in the happy position of being a somewhat autocratic Dean, carrying his Chapter with him and having little or no interference from his diocesan. Now he thought that the bishop should have a larger part to play in the life of the Cathedral than merely occupying his *cathedra* when the occasion required. He made some tentative moves in this direction but was defeated by a resolute Dean and Chapter. One weekday morning he ordered a change of vestments, not wishing to use those that had been laid out for him. He then received a letter, respectful but firm, requesting that in future he would conform to usage of the Cathedral. He then suggested that on those Sundays when he was not otherwise engaged, he, as bishop, ought to be the celebrant at the principal Eucharist at the Cathedral. The Dean and Chapter informed him that this was not practicable. The Cathedral clergy had insufficient opportunities to preside at the Eucharist on Sundays, and the Dean, as vicar of the parish, already had too few opportunities to meet his parishioners at the altar. At the time a new chapel, designed by George Pace, was nearing completion at Llys Esgob, and so Glyn replied, almost in despair : "When I get my chapel, it seems that I must restrict myself to it."

Another matter on which Glyn wrote to the Dean and Chapter was the Llandaff Festival. He had some reservations about the use of the Cathedral for this important artistic event, as it had already become, but the answer he received countered all the points which he had raised. The Visitation enabled him to have the last word on this subject and to voice the doubts that he still retained. He admitted that earlier days, when there was a less rigid line drawn between the secular and the sacred, provided some precedent for the growing use of cathedrals for concerts, plays, festivals and so forth :

> But the very fact that the Christian religion has not now the influence it did should warn us against too easy a supposition that activities of this kind somehow exert an evangelistic influence or make the Cathedral an effective spiritual force. Certainly I am somewhat disconcerted to have people congratulate me on having a "full Cathedral" for, say, one of the events of the Llandaff Festival, as if this was somehow equivalent to an unusually large number of communicants, say at Easter or Christmas. It suggests that perhaps not so much of what a cathedral really is all about is carried over by these events as one hopes.

The General Charge to the diocese covered a wide variety of subjects. Then came a summing up :

> As I look at the picture of the diocese as it has revealed itself to me in preparing this Charge, it has many sombre shades. Clerical manpower continues to decline ; we have 222 priests in our parishes as compared with 301 thirty years ago ; Easter communicants continue to decline ; so do the numbers baptized and confirmed, and the number of regular worshippers in our churches; more, perhaps many more churches may have to be closed. On the other hand £165,000 has been spent on church extension, restoration and maintenance; £100,000 on parsonage houses and about the same amount on schools ; £70,000 for overseas work, all in the last five years. Probably it would have

been a better sign of health if the first and last of these figures had been reversed. But at least they indicate life and the potentiality of more. There is need for a realistic grasp of the situation, but for idealism as well.

Both realism and idealism lay ahead in the shape of the report of the Diocesan Commission which was expected by the following Easter : "When the time comes I look to an end of complacency and meaningless conservatism, as I look also to an absence of policies suggested by slogans rather than by serious study, and of a passion for change merely for its own sake."

Meanwhile other changes were being made. At the April meeting of the Governing Body Glyn had the task of presenting the draft revised service of the Holy Eucharist. This seemed a momentous step at the time. In this case, unlike the other experimental services, it was decided to have a preliminary discussion about it before going on to seek permission for its experimental use. It was necessary to convince the members of the Governing Body that there was a need for this revision of the familiar Prayer Book service, and this Glyn did very tellingly.

Largely for controversial reasons the primitive pattern of Christian worship was broken up and confused. The simplicity of its structure was distorted by the introduction of mainly devotional and personal accretions and pieces of edification which have their place but not at the cost of obscuring the common pattern of worship. The Reformers were strongly under the influence of St. Augustine at his darkest, and were almost obsessed by human guilt ; hence the introduction of lengthy and sombre acts of repentance in which the loving Father seems to have disappeared before the stern judge; hence too the frequent and often lengthy exhortations which further confused the service. One of the gravest results of all this may be explained in the words of some Rhondda teenagers who had attended a Choral Eucharist. Asked what they thought, they said : "It was alright ; but is'nt it a sad service ?" A sad service ! Something has gone very wrong when this can be said of a service which at first was full of joy, when even the Cross itself, central as it is, was only seen wreathed in the light of Easter, so that when men gazed upon the figure upon it, they saw him only as reigning from the Tree, King of Glory and of Peace. The revision before us goes a long way to bring all this to the fore.

The Report of the Llandaff Diocesan Commission appeared in print in 1968. Glyn had submitted five questions to the Commission which had divided itself into five sub-committees to deal with those questions. The answers covered the major part of the life of the diocese from the work of the priest and the function of the laity to the more mundane matters of parish boundaries and surplus buildings. The Commission had worked hard and there was some disappointment at the lack of immediate and practical results. But it needs time for reforms such as those which the Commission recommended to be put into effect ; and time was not on Glyn's side. He had at most but five years before compulsory retirement. Also he was becoming conscious of a nervous disorder, later to be diagnosed as Parkinson's Disease. In the year that the printed report came out, he was elected Archbishop of Wales. It was a challenge that he could not but accept ; but it was a decision which worried him not a little.

"His tragedy was that it was entirely the wrong move ... the Archbishopric was a constraint within which his particular gifts could not be used to the full."[24] Such is the verdict of a recent commentator on the history of the Church in Wales. Having stated that Glyn was "at his peak as Bishop of Llandaff between 1957 and 1968", the writer clearly considered the brief period as Archbishop to be something of an anti-climax. It must be admitted that Glyn seemed to become obsessed with domestic matters, the Welsh language and bilingual road signs, whereas formerly he had concentrated on wider issues. And as the pigs in *Animal Farm* eventually approximated to human appearance, so Glyn became increasingly like those he had formerly despised, the "safe" clergymen who sat on the committees and commissions (and electoral colleges) of the Church in Wales. But the verdict is an over-simplification. The old fire remained though it had but a short time to burn.

8

ARCHBISHOP OF WALES

The Induction and Installation of the sixth Archbishop of Wales took place in Llandaff Cathedral 17 July 1968. The newspapers were quick to point out that Glyn had "made history by being the first man to be elected Archbishop without being the senior bishop at the time". He himself remarked in retrospect : "It was no doubt the will of the great majority that I should become Archbishop ; but if Edwin Morris had retired earlier it would not have been easy to pass over the Bishop of St. Asaph (the senior bishop), good, kind, diligent David Bartlett, a man of peace and love."

In the following September Glyn was seen to be Archbishop when he presided over the Governing Body. This, Archbishop Green declared, is "the organ through which the common mind of the Church in Wales becomes articulate". But the means to that end are sometimes trying, as Glyn remarked in his parish magazine in 1951 : "Surrounding the Governing Body's meetings on Wednesday and Thursday was the buzzing of innumerable committees which left us exhausted by Friday morning ; but alas, nobody was stung into life or death ; preferably the latter." And indeed the Governing Body has gone its ponderous way year after year, receiving the reports of a steadily increasing number of committees and commissions which may be important but are not always exciting.

The Ordinary Meeting of the Governing Body is the occasion for the President's address. In 1968 Glyn chose the subject, ' Wales, the Welsh Language and the Church '. It reflects his historical interests though sometimes he was too much of a partisan to be a detached historian ; it also indicates his views on the contemporary situation in Wales and the direction in which the new Archbishop hoped to lead the Church.

He began by saying that the ancient Church in this land had been taken in hand and reshaped by the Norman conquerors. There had been great gains, but also heavy losses, for thee strangement of Welsh tithes and endowments for the benefit of monasteries founded by the Normans "laid the foundation for the poverty of the Welsh Church which has persisted to this day".

Despite the considerable indifference of the Roman authorities (no Welshman was bishop of Llandaff for two centuries before the Reformation, for example) Wales remained a country devoutly Catholic, ministered to by Welsh-speaking priests and strengthened by devotion to the old native saints. When the Reformation came it made little or no appeal to Wales. The disappearance of many popular and revered customs was much resented and very unpopular. The appearance of English services was greeted with extreme disfavour. "Latin I know and Welsh I speak," wrote an indignant Welsh squire near Swansea, "but this English I cannot manage." "Ffydd Saeson" —the "English religion" soon became a current and unpopular term. Many Welshmen went to the stake rather than accept it. Prophets might reasonably have forecast that Wales would go the way of Ireland. Why did this not happen ?

It must be said that there is no conclusive historical evidence to support these bland statements. The changes that took place in Wales during the Refromation were accepted without demur; and historians to this day can only speculate as to the reasons. Glyn continued with the traditional answer to his question.

It did not happen because of Elizabeth's sympathy with Wales and her appointment and encouragement of Welsh-speaking bishops and clergy. These men, like Bishop Richard Davies and Bishop William Morgan, set to work as early as 1567 to translate the Book of Common Prayer and the Bible into Welsh as well as to provide handbooks of popular devotion in the same language, thus laying the foundation of modern Welsh press and literature . . . Language and history and church were identified. The Welshman found in Church and Monarchy, through a romantic attachment to the Tudor dynasty which was transferred to the Stuarts, a source of loyalty, a cause which survived the Commonwealth and persisted, but with slowly dying zeal, through the days of the unattractive Hanoverians down to the Methodist Revival in Wales . . . Welsh people became divided in language and the attachment of the bulk of the people to the Church, though it persisted, became more and more formal until it finally collapsed before the powerful Welsh preachers of the Methodist Revival.

Thus far Glyn had faithfully expounded that "Methodist" history of Wales "which has been accepted uncritically to a very surprising extent by Churchmen no less than Nonconformists". It can be summarized as follows. The pre-Reformation Church was very popular in Wales. The post-Reformation Church was and remained an alien and unpopular institution. The Restoration and Hanoverian Church sank to untold depths of apathy and corruption. Finally the darkness passed and the day dawned with the coming of the Methodist Revival. There are some elements of truth in all this but, it has been said, "there are also serious and basic misconceptions embodied in it and it badly needs revision".[25] Some reinterpretation had already taken place but the speaker seemed unaware of it. He was on firmer ground when he came to the modern period.

Thus were laid the foundations of the Nonconformist supremacy in Wales which permeated every aspect of it for a century and a half. It imposed upon Wales a pattern known as "the Welsh way of life", by which must be understood life as lived in pious Nonconformist homes, puritan, protestant, teetotal, sabbatarian and Welsh-speaking. In this way walked until recently the great majority of the professors, bank managers, doctors . . . substantial farmers and shopkeepers of Wales, as well as the great Welsh drapers and milk retailers of London. Over against them stood the old Church of the land, the Church of an aristocracy and gentry completely English in upbringing and outlook, the Church of the great English immigration that industrialisation brought to Wales, but also still the Church of a Welsh-speaking minority which included scholarly Welsh clerics who kept alive the Welsh literary tradition in the days when the Methodists thought nothing of it ; the Church, too, of the poor and the feckless, so seldom at home with puritans. Now the pattern is changing ; the decline in Nonconformity is marked ; there is respect and even affection for the now disestablished Church which nevertheless faces, though perhaps in different ways, the same crisis as the Free Churches. It seems unlikely that we shall solve it alone though we have special problems and probably in some respects different solutions.

This was a period of revived national spirit in Wales as in other parts of the world but "there is nothing unscriptural or un-Christian in nationalism as such". Glyn went on to say that nationalism needs to be disciplined and purified. There was no room for dangerous acts of violence or for "ignorant discourtesy to a young man who is in no way responsible for the position in which he finds himself"—this was the year before the Investiture of the Prince of Wales—but the speaker came down firmly in favour of devolution :

> Wales is not a region but a nation, and a nation without political institutions of her own, while an increasingly centralised Government makes the appreciation of her special problems difficult to apprehend or solve. It is difficult to see why what is good enough for Northern Ireland or Scotland or the Isle of Man, to say nothing of Southern Ireland, is not good enough for Wales . . . It is also vital to realise that on this political question Wales is far from united, and disunity and quarrels and bitterness are very near the surface on both sides when the question is mooted.

From nationalism he turned to the subject of language. History had made Wales a bilingual country, and understanding was needed on both sides if lasting damage was to be avoided. If there was not to be a division based on language, there must be a genuine bilingual policy in Wales, with parity of esteem and usage for both languages at all levels. He ended with an appeal that the Church in Wales should be a Church of understanding for *all* her children ; and the italics were his.

Glyn had told the Governing Body that the Government had begun to make some moves towards giving equality of status to the Welsh language, but its progress was still slow. Preaching at St. David's Roman Catholic Cathedral in 1969 at a Civic Service attended by the Lord Mayor of Cardiff, Alderman Lincoln Hallinan, he stated that those who spoke Welsh, "when they visit their capital city have the right to see their native language having its proper place in official documents and on official occasions, and to be able to find their way about by means of sign boards and notices in their own tongue". But he could not resist the aside, inspired by the dedication of the Cathedral, that the Welsh Saints "were no social reformers ; they did not lead a kind of primitive teetotal movement ; they did not preside at Eisteddfodau or commit themselves to ardent nationalistic sentiments ; they stood for God and his righteousness". Yet his espousal of the cause of bilingualism in Wales was consistent and sincere.

About this time the members of the Welsh Language Society intensified their campaign against anglicised place-names by daubing paint over the offending "barbarian" forms. In April 1969 some of them were dealt with rather severely in a North Wales court and Glyn was moved to write a letter of protest to the *Western Mail*.

> All of us to whom the support of the Law is important will have felt it inevitable that those who disfigure road signs should be punished. But many Welshmen must have read of the fines inflicted at Betws y Coed with mixed feelings. Law, to retain the respect of the people, must not be unreasonable or appear to be unjust. Many of us feel that it is right and proper that in a bilingual country signposts and such like should be in both languages. Welsh-speaking Welshmen do not speak of Tenby or Swansea or Bridgend ; they use the Welsh names. Surely it is not unreasonable that they should expect to see these names on the signposts of their country.

In the following year Glyn paid a visit, which received a good deal of publicity, to the Chairman of the Welsh Language Society, Dafydd Iwan, when the latter was in Cardiff Gaol for refusing to pay a fine.

Dafydd Iwan recalls that the visit of the Archbishop of Wales, due to its unprecedented nature, posed not a few problems for the Governor of the Gaol. It came as a complete surprise to the language campaigner who now met Glyn for the first time. He found that his visitor was very easy to talk to, and certainly did not give the impression that he was doing anything out of the ordinary. Glyn was concerned about the status of the Welsh language, as he had already made clear that an Archbishop of Wales should be. He agreed with the aims if not always the methods of the Welsh Language Society. He therefore wanted to find out more about them, and to add his weight to the struggle for the recognition of the Welsh language. He was not concerned in the least about any adverse publicity he might receive. Dafydd Iwan, on whom this visit made a lasting impression, concluded that his visitor was a man who, if he thought he should do something, went boldly on without any fear of criticism.[26]

There were many who wondered whether the Archbishop

should involve himself in matters which had political overtones ; but Glyn was unrepentant. He spoke about bilingual roadsigns again at the Urdd Eisteddfod of 1971 and received a great ovation for his uncompromising words.

At the Investiture of the Prince of Wales in Caernarfon Castle 1 July 1969 there was a short service in which the Archbishop took part. It was apparent that Glyn's nervous disorder was getting worse for the hand that rested on the lectern was shaking and the episcopal ring beat a steady tattoo which was picked up by the microphones and broadcast to every listener. Yet he was as active as ever and on a second visit to America he had found that Wales was now very much on the map. He referred to this in a lecture to the Honourable Society of Cymmrodorion 21 April 1970.

> There has been a most interesting development in the U.S.A. When I was there six or seven years ago there was almost complete ignorance of Wales, even in Pennsylvania, even in places called Radnor or Bala Cynwyd ; one had to explain it from the beginning. When I visited the States again last year the position was completely changed. There was an almost embarrassing thirst for information ; every third house seemed to have records of Welsh choirs singing hymns . . . This was entirely due to the Prince of Wales and his Investiture.

In this lecture Glyn roused the ire of admirers of Lloyd George when he said that Welshmen would have to live with the fact that many Englishmen had their doubts about them : "There is more than a suggestion of shiftiness to deal with, a reputation for being circuitous or tortuous, for being slick, for being too clever by half, for brilliance founded on nothing very solid. I have no doubt that we have Lloyd George much to thank for this . . . It is the penalty of having provided Great Britain, in a time first of social change and then of deadly peril, with a great man in whom we can see our national virtues and failings on a large scale." He then went on to expound his view of the national character :

> The real explanation of our undoubted deviousness is pretty simple : several centuries of war and conquest, of poverty and deprivation, forced us to live by our wits, so that even when this is no longer necessary we avoid a straight answer if we can.

127

We create for ourselves endless trouble by complicated man-
oeuvres when the straight way is not only obvious but free
of trouble. Coupled with this are two other characteristics—
the desire to please, or at least to avoid giving obvious hurt.
The other is the capacity for believing intensely in what one
is saying at the moment, without intending to do anything
about it, and quite possibly being unaware that one is not
intending to do anything about it, by even passing on to another
perhaps contradictory subject almost immediately and pro-
claiming that too with equal eloquence and conviction. Small
wonder that all this, set in a composite vague memory of the
course of Welsh history—mixed up with Caradoc Evans'
novels, "How Green is my Valley", Richard Burton, ardent
and eloquent trade union leaders, elusive outside-halves, Under
Milkwood—presents to the Anglo-Saxon mind a perspective
so bewildering as to be instinctively mistrusted.

There is some flippancy here, but it was too serious an occasion
merely to jest. Glyn himself could be very devious and he
cheerfully admitted it. These words are probably a compound
of self-examination and observation of others. Besides , he had
already stated that it was high time the Welsh were proud of
their nation, "not self-consciously or aggressively, but quietly
and simply, as people content to be judged on their record and
to let it speak for itself".

Soon after his installation as Archbishop Glyn attended his
second Lambeth Conference. It was larger than usual for not
only diocesan but suffragan and assistant bishops were present.
This time he was secretary to a Section whose subject was
' Renewal in Faith '. There were fourteen sub-sections and he
had to act "as a kind of editor and precis maker of these sub-
committee's reports, often under tremendous pressure". Large
contingents of bishops from America, Canada and Australia
had given a strong Anglo-Saxon flavour to the Conference ;
but this was balanced by a considerable increase in the number
of bishops native to various parts of the world, and their presence made him "very much aware of the developing countries
and of the religions there with which these Christian bishops
had to contend". He returned to home and diocese "feeling
very much like a kind of Rip Van Winkle returning to a world
I seemed to have lost years ago". In the following November
he was at Canterbury delivering a carefully prepared lecture

on ' Presenting Christian Faith '. The main theme was to defend rationally the evidence for the life and teaching of the Lord Jesus : "It is our duty to recognise the need for reinterpretation of the Christian Faith in each age. It is our duty to recognise the special difficulties which make the Faith hard to accept in an age of unparalleled technological and scientific achievement." Therefore, as at Durham some years before, he advocated a spirit of humility and a readiness to say : "I do not know."

Soon there was a second visit to America. At the Trinity Institute in New York he dilated on his favourite subject, ' Bishops '. He largely covered familiar ground, except for the remark : "It is contrary to the genius of the Anglican episcopate to go in for heresy hunts ; Gamaliel is or should be their patron saint."

In 1970 the Church in Wales celebrated the fiftieth anniversary of its Disestablishment and Disendowment, and on 9 January the *Church Times* published Glyn's reflections on the life of the Province during these years.

> To the tidy Norman mind the way in which the Church in Wales carried on was exasperating and they lost no time in putting things right. In August 1107 Urban, the first Norman bishop of Llandaff, was consecrated by Anselm, the Archbishop of Canterbury, and the first step was taken to incorporate the Welsh Church into the Province of Canterbury of which it was to remain an integral part until in 1920 it became an independent province of its own. An entirely new way of Church life had to be devised, and years were spent before 1920 preparing a new method of Church government and new financial arrangements . . . The bishops were excluded from the House of Lords, but Archbishop Edwards could still be seen from time to time, sitting on the steps of the Lord Chancellor's seat, surveying the scene of many an impassioned battle. Removed from Convocation, the Welsh bishops were invited to share in the bishops' meetings in London, and did so almost to a man until recently when the problems discussed there seemed increasingly to be relevant to the particular situation in England, and to an Established Church in particular . . . Free to produce its own Book of Common Prayer, the new Province took over the 1662 Book, and in 1928, under the strongly Protestant lead of Archbishop Edwards, roundly refused to touch the Revised Book . . .

He then went on to describe in detail the working of the Constitution of the Church in Wales :

A Representative Body of bishops, priests and laymen, as holder of all Church property with its own seal, took the place of corporations aggregate such as Deans and Chapters or Parochial Church Councils, and of corporations sole, such as bishops, or perpetual curates (none of whom now survive in Wales, though from time to time letters from some Church of England lawyer surprise the vicar of some former corporation of this kind by writing to him under his old title). The Parson's Freehold has gone, too, but those in England who are nervous of the consequences of this may be reassured. It is just as difficult to move a clergyman without it as with it.

Glyn described the working of the Governing Body, the method of electing bishops and the new methods of patronage, now in the hands of the bishops and the diocesan and provincial boards; for with Disestablishment, private patrons of every kind disappeared. He then referred to the results of Disendowment. About three and a half million pounds had been secularised:

The Cathedrals suffered through the disappearance of residentiary canonries providing opportunities for study. Learning and special skills, hitherto given their chance in small but well-endowed benefices, also suffered, and only very recently has there been a recognition of the necessity of specialist as distinct from parochial ministries. The absence of such posts (and financial pressures will prevent them ever being numerous) is one reason for clergy from Wales seeking posts in Canterbury and York. Other causes, some good and some bad, account for many others, to such an extent that Wales may almost be said to be for the Church of England the tribe of Levi that Ireland is for the Church of Rome.

A survey of the present activities of the Church in Wales, the work of its Liturgical Commission, its university chaplaincies, its work with youth and with church schools ended with the remark : "We are old-fashioned enough to maintain two Retreat Houses, one in St. Davids and one in Llandaff." Then Glyn turned his attention to the general state of things in Wales :

The present situation of organised Christianity in Wales, though less critical in some ways than it is elsewhere, is still pretty grim. Scores of chapels have been closed all over Wales, though certainly more frequently in the industrial than in the rural areas. Not many of their worshippers have transferred to the Parish Church, for their ethos is still that of Protestant Nonconformity, unsupernatural, undogmatic, unsacramental in theology, starkly "puritan" in morality, concentrating on drink, sex and gambling as the really great sins. Unfortuntely the Church, in the heyday of the Welsh chapels, only too often paid them the compliment of imitation. There exists a great spiritual vacuum in Wales and someone or something sooner or later will certainly fill it. Will it be the ancient Church of the land ? There is much to discourage us, but I am full of hope, even though things may, and almost certainly will, get worse before they are better. The Church in Wales stands today in Ezekiel's valley of dry bones, "very many and very dry". And sometimes we say, "Can these dry bones live ?" We can hardly believe that they can. But God says : "I will put my spirit upon you and you shall live." All who love the Church, and, at this anniversary of its Disestablishment, the Church in Wales in particular, must pray that God will not speak in vain, and that we shall be ready to follow wherever the Spirit leads.

When describing the origin of the Governing Body of the Church in Wales, Glyn quoted from Archbishop Green's book, *The Constitution of the Church in Wales in its Setting* : "It is important to remember that the Governing Body did not come into being as a result of consultations and conferences of the clergy and laity. Its creation resulted from a summons by the bishops." In giving approval to this rather fine distinction, Glyn succumbed to the temptation of following the authority of Archbishop Green without any regard for changed or changing circumstances or ideas, as he himself said.

The influence of Dr. Green's book, which was compulsory reading for a whole generation of Welsh clergymen, has been, to say the least, unfortunate. His doctrine of episcopacy is that of a late nineteenth century Anglo-Catholic. Authoritarian in the extreme, it is based on a mechanical view of the Apostolic Succession—rather reminiscent of charging a new battery from the electric mains—which has long been outmoded. He was one of the framers of the new Constitution of the Church in Wales ; but perhaps he found himself in uncongenial company, for Glyn wrote :

131

Two other distinguished judges, Lord Atkin an Sir John Bankes, made considerable contributions. They were essentially Erastian in their outlook and Atkin in particular tended to see the Church, even as disestablished, as a department of State and was suspicious of episcopal authority.

Green had the last word for the Constitution contains phrases which read : "no proceeding of the Governing Body shall interfere with the excercise by the Archbishop of the powers and functions inherent in the Office of Metropolitan, nor with the exercise by the Diocesan Bishops of the powers and functions inherent in the Episcopal Office. But the Constitution is uncertain on this point. It seems only to allow the diocesan bishop to do what the Governing Body of the Church in Wales allows him to do. The procedure adopted for liturgical revision provides an example. The Constiution of the Church in Wales requires that alterations to the Book of Common Prayer must be made by bill procedure at the Governing Body ; and normally the bill must have the backing of a majority of the Order of Bishops. The use of revised services for an experimental period had not been envisaged by the framers of the Constitution, and so it was deemed necessary to steer a bill through the Governing Body to allow for this new development. Promulgated as a Canon in 1955 the relevant clauses read :

1. A Diocesan Bishop shall have power to authorise for experimental use in the churches within his diocese any proposed revisions of a part or parts of the Book of Common Prayer which have been provisionally approved by the Bench of Bishops . . . provided that the Governing Body shall have assented to the experimental use of the proposed revisions without alteration.

2. A Diocesan Bishop shall not take action under Clause I hereof until after the next meeting of the Governing Body following the circulation to members of the Governing Body of printed copies of the proposed revision.

These words could be taken to imply that the Governing Body confers authority on the diocesan bishop. Alternatively, it could be said that the Canon spells out the bishop's *ius liturgicum*, but then immediately limits it by requiring that the bishop acts in conjunction with his fellows ; and that the Governing Body must be invited to assent and have assented to their corporate action. One is tempted to wonder if this is what Green intended; or indeed to ask if this is episcopacy? There seems to be an indefinable something above the diocesan bishop, as though Green and his fellows have wished upon the Church in Wales a refined form of papacy. Whether the "pope" is the Governing Body or the Bench of Bishops, or indeed both, is open to debate.

Glyn often used to say that the Welsh bishops "worked together" and he often used to speak of bishops having a collective responsibility. This may well have been his contribution to the ongoing search which has to be made by the Archbishops of Wales, no less than others, for their true selves or for the *ethos* of their office.

In 1920 the Archbishop of Wales had to start, as it were, from the beginning. The examples of other parts of the Anglican Communion did not help much, for as Glyn once sagely remarked : "It is difficult to think of a typical disestablished Church : each one is *sui generis*." A. G. Edwards, however, was too old a dog to learn new tricks. He had, after all, been a bishop of the Established Church for too long a time to change his ways when he became the archbishop of a disestablished Province. Therefore he carried on as before. His successor, Archbishop Green, provided the Archbishopric with a *raison d'etre*. He began, as Glyn has told us, with the conviction that he was "a bishop of the Catholic Church, and that triumphed over all else". Green had seen the State remove the privileges which belonged to the Establishment ; yet nothing, in his eyes, could alter the fact that he was the Metropolitan of the Catholic Church in the land of Wales, that Church which stretched in unbroken succession from the Age of the Saints. The Law of the Land might no longer apply, but Canon Law made up for all the deficiencies. This, in brief, was the thesis of Green's book on the Constiution of the Church in Wales,. His natural aloofness and his sense of grandeur provided a suitable background for this theology. He set a pattern which was all too well maintained, in particular by Archbishop John Morgan who continued the Green tradition to a nicety. Nor was Archbishop Morris unaffected by it. In 1946, as Bishop of Monmouth, he held his first Visitation and he told his clergy : "As incumbents you have a ministry to all the souls in your parishes; this includes Roman Catholics and Nonconformists as well as the unbaptized." The statement caused no little stir at the time. The Bishop, however, with characteristic determination, returned to the same theme in his second Visitation Charge, substantiating his claim from the XXXIX Articles, the Canons of 1603, the Book of Common Prayer, the Ordinal, and the Constitution of the Church in Wales. Both in object and in method this was the triumph of the Green tradition.

Glyn realised that changed and changing circumstances had overtaken the Green tradition. In the 1960s it seemed quite out of date. It was far too medieval in *ethos*. It was not the way to commend episcopacy in an ecumenical age. He therefore looked back to a more primitive pattern, and concentrated attention on the liturgical and pastoral aspects of the bishop's office. The natural corollary was to think that the bishop's funtions would be exercised most effectively not by one but by a college of bishops. In his second Visitiation Charge at Llandaff he said :

> It seems plain that a new pattern, or rather the recovery of an old pattern, of the bishop's ministry is required. Could it be brought about by the creation within this diocese of two or even three other bishops ? Not suffragan or assistant bishops, but bishops with a cathedral and jurisdiction of their own, meeting together as a college every month and dividing between them the episcopal duties and privileges that now fall on one.

These ideas seemed to have influenced the Archbishop's Commission on the Boundaries and Structures of the Church in Wales set up by Glyn himself in 1970. But the modest proposals for collegiate episcopacy, contained in the Commission's Report, were firmly rejected by the Governing Body in 1980.

During this year there was a good deal of running about to be done in the Province and many opportunities to reflect upon the past. The Church of Ireland was also marking the Centenary of its Disestablishment and on 17 March Glyn was preaching in St. Patrick's Cathedral, Armagh. This time he had something to say about other results of disestablishment in Wales :

The Disestablishment Campaign was only partially inspired by religion ; its origins and its continual inspiration were more social and political. When it came to an end with the passing of the Welsh Church Act in 1920 the fire went out in the Non-conformist pulpit, and in politics the Liberal Party in Wales, which had made Welsh Church Disestablishment its major interest, lost its impetus and finally disappeared, except where Welsh conservatism, an interesting phenomenon in what had become politically a radical nation, preserved its remnants for another twenty-five years or so in parliamentary seats associated with Mr. Lloyd George and his family.

Not only in Wales but also in the United Kingdom, the Liberal Party which had been the instrument of disestablishment in Ireland as well as Wales was by 1920 in fragments, broken by war, social change, and personal antagonisms. Before the war Conservatives and Liberals had been divided on such great questions as Ireland, the Franchise, the Church and the Land. Now all these issues had gone. 1920 was the beginning of a new epoch not only for the Church in Wales but also for British politics.

The Governing Body in 1969 accepted Glyn's proposal that the Jubilee of the Province of Wales should be marked by an appeal to all its members to contribute one day's pay for relief overseas. The Feast of the Patron Saint of Wales, 1 March 1970, was the obvious choice for the date. The amount contributed —nearly £47,000—was a good deal less than what had been expected ; but Glyn was not unduly disappointed, as he wrote in his Diocesan Leaflet :

> The result is roughly what I expected, though others were much more optimistic and have been rather cast down in consequence . . . Many people thought we should make a big campaign of it but I did not want this. I wanted a short sharp appeal and response, and the literature sent out should have been quite enough to indicate the needs which prompted the appeal. Disestablishment took place fifty years ago and we must look to the future. This will call amongst other things for a much wider view of the Gospel and the Church if, under God, anything creative is to emerge. It is just here that the objections to the aims of the appeal, which led many to refuse to support it, are most terrifying. "Where there is no vision the people perish."

The time was, in fact, too short. St. David's Day came too early in the year despite the valiant attempt of Church in Wales Publications to get the literature out in time ; but he was probably right in wanting the appeal to be short and sharp.

Glyn's third and final Charge to the diocese of Llandaff was not published. It was his valediction, and in it he took stock of the situation in the diocese whose oversight he had undertaken with high hopes some fourteen years before.

> I must begin this Charge, as I did the two which preceded it, with an expression of my deep gratitude to all in this diocese who work so hard and in so many ways for the Church into which we were all baptized. The phrase "who have worked so hard" must be held to imply not mere physical or mental or spiritual labour. It must often be taken to include in it such elements as disappointment and frustration in the setting in which they work, the sometimes grinding task of keeping going expensive buildings, awareness of the growing separation be-tween Church and people, including some of their most loved and respected friends who simply cannot see the relevance of the Church or even of Christianity to their everyday lives. Then there are the frequent reports in the Press and elsewhere of utterances or books written mostly by men of wide knowledge of out of the way or bygone aspects of the Christian Faith. The average man who sits lightly to the demands of his religion is not to know how unbalanced and personal such displays are, or how little weight they are given by genuine New Testament and Church historians. But they add to the perplexity of the faithful, for whom it is not an easy matter to put up with snippets or newspaper articles or broadcast interviews of this kind, quoted to them with the suggestion that there is really no need to take the Church or the Christian Faith seriously any longer. I have little doubt that many whose Christianity has long been nom-inal, represented by an attendance at worship only at Christmas and Easter no longer keep even this slender link with the Church of their childhood. Easter communicants have declined not only because so many people are now constantly on the move, but also because the gap between committed Christians and occasional visitors to Church services is now much wider . . . Nevertheless the growing rejection of the Christian Faith is a very serious matter which lies behind most of the problems of what is often called a Permissive Society. An older generation of Christians used to argue against those who claimed to accept Christian morality while rejecting Christian dogma. Reject Christian dogma, they used to say, and Christian

morality will never survive,. This seems to have been uncomfortably near the mark.

He was concerned about the effect of the sceptical climate of opinion upon the clergy. It had already hit the Roman Catholic Church particularly hard "and priests of the Church have abandoned their calling and sometimes their faith in numbers which must cause dismay amongst their leaders". A similar phenomenon could be discerned in the Ministry of the Free Churches "and it did not follow that all is happiness and content with the Welsh clergy". He urged the need for refresher courses for the clergy which, he thought, would be welcomed by the great majority with deep gratitude and profound relief. Then he concluded :

> We do not believe that the Christian Faith and Christian Theology are collapsing around us. We believe that Truth is in it; indeed that He is in it who is the Way, the Truth, and the Life. But we need to see him better and to hear his word and to have the opportunity to live his life, here and now in times of change.

For the first time the prophetic voice had faltered. For the first time in a public pronouncement there had been no confident challenge to the ills of the age. The strain of office and worsening health were taking their toll.

The decision to retire had already been taken and on 5 April 1971 Glyn had written to the senior bishop :

> In accordance with Chapter VIII Sections 28 and 31 of the Constitution of the Church in Wales I place my resignation as Archbishop and as Bishop in your hands, the former to take effect on 30 June next, and the latter to take effort on 31 August . I am sorry to have to take these steps, but, largely owing to the effect of Parkinson's Disease, I can no longer concentrate on the many difficult decisions which lie before us, to say nothing of the careful reading, which is essential, of the numerous documents which now shower upon us all. Had I known, or even received a hint, that I had this disease at the time the archbishop's Electoral College met, I should have refused the Office, but apparently it was neither known or guessed at. Two doctors gave me a clean bill of health. The enclosed letter, which I have sent to leading laity, goes a little more fully into things.

The relevant part of the second letter read :

> As you know, I am suffering from Parkinson's Disease. The drugs I am taking will, I hope, prevent it from extending. They have greatly improved my writing, which at one time was so bad that I could not even sign my name without a struggle. They have also improved my voice which at one time was very difficult to manage. But my mind and thinking are still impaired, and my memory and powers of concentration affected. In the very critical and complicated stage in which the Church, and everything else, is today, it would be fatal if the Archbishop was not able to cope, or worse still, cope inadequately. I hope I am not letting anyone down, but I do not think I am ; it would be pleasant to carry on, but the risks are too great ; at times I feel quite unwell . . . I did hope to be able to carry on with Llandaff, but I just can't. We have found ourselves a home, in what were the servants' quarters of a great Georgian rectory in Somerset, in a very small village called Goathurst, with part of the parish church almost in the kitchen.

He was able to use the word "we" in the letter because in the previous year he had married again. His wife, formerly Mrs. Camellia Rees, was the widow of Trevor Pritchard Rees, the grandson of the founder of the firm of Noah Rees, the Cardiff Agricultural Merchants. She lived in Llandaff and had been a close friend of Sheila Simon. They were married in St. Peter's, Carmarthen, 2 February 1970, and the service was conducted by the Incumbent, Canon D. Hywel Davies, Glyn's brother-in-law. Hywel was an undergraduate at the Univesity of North Wales and a resident in the Church Hostel when he first met his future wife, Esther Simon. Later he was successively vicar of Monkton and Carmarthen.

"Cam", as she is known to her friends, was a tower of strength to her husband during the busy year of 1970. In March they were welcoming the then Archbishop of York and Mrs. Coggan to Llandaff on the occasion of the service at Llandaff Cathedral to mark the reception in Wales of the New English Bible. Not long afterwards they were being entertained at Canterbury by Dr. and Mrs. Michael Ramsey when Glyn was due to preach at the Cathedral. In July they were in Swansea where Glyn received an honorary doctorate of the

University of Wales. Besides these were the many events concerned with the jubilee of the independence of the Church in Wales. Then in 1971 they had to face the difficult decision about retirement. What settled it in Glyn's mind was his desire to be remembered as a "standing up" Archbishop. He did not want his people, and in particular his confirmation candidates, to think of him as the Archbishop with the shaking hand. They found the Dower House at Goathurst almost by accident when they were staying near Taunton with one of their friends. Now it was time to say goodbye to a whole host of people. The farewell dinners were eaten, the presentations made and the regrets expressed, and they moved into their new house towards the end of August. There was one further presentation which gave Glyn much pleasure. It was a miner's lamp on which was inscribed : "Presented to Dr. Glyn Simon by the South Wales Coal Industry Social Welfare Organisation in recognition of his services to the miners, 20 November 1971."

The days at Goathurst passed very happily. Glyn occasionally preached or celebrated the Holy Eucharist in the parish church. On St. David's Day 1972 he asked permission to use the experimental Welsh Rite and this was readily granted. The surrounding area enabled him to indulge his tastes in ecclesiology ; and he had another interest which was eminently suitable for life in the country. He had been a life-long student of ornithology and was familiar with many learned monographs on the subject. He had two new step-sons, Bruce Rees, a Metallurgist at the Llanwern Steelworks, and Colin, a Zoologist working in America. Colin had grown up in Llandaff and became an admirer of his Bishop for the resolute stand taken by the latter on social and racial problems. When he came over from America in 1970 he was much impressed by his step-father's scientific knowledge and they had long conversations on subjects which they had in common. Colin brought to Llandaff his wife and their new baby whom Glyn christened Trevor Pritchard in memory of the infant's grandfather.

A holiday in Italy in April 1972 was almost a reunion for the Simon family. Robin was teaching in Italy, and Perpetua was also there on a working holiday. Only Nicholas remained in this country, working at the Department of the Environment and unable to join them. Glyn's health seemed to be improving and he was all the better for the peace of Goathurst and the sunshine of Italy. One holiday memory in particular gave him much joy. During his stay in Verona he had been allowed to celebrate the Holy Eucharist in the crypt of one of the most important churches there. Robin recalls that his father felt the significance of this (clandestine) act of ecumenism very deeply : "Coming at the end of his life, and at the time I last saw him, its importance seems even greater."

As the result of a sudden illness Glyn was admitted to Musgrove Park Hospital, Taunton, on Saturday 10 June. On the following Tuesday he had a heart attack. Later that day he was able to receive the Holy Communion, administered by the Hospital Chaplain and some hours later he was anointed. Next day he appeared to be much better, but another heart attack in the afternoon proved to be fatal. His body rested in the parish church at Goathurst before being taken to Llandaff Cathedral for the Requiem and for the funeral service on Monday 19 June 1972.

At the end of the manuscript reminiscences which he wrote at Goathurst Glyn set down some brief but illuminating comments about himself. They are probably the last words that he wrote, and he looked back over his life as though he sensed that his time was short.

"I was never a popular clergyman in the sense of having a ' following' ; and I was for years (and I suspect in some cases right up to the end of my time) considered a liablility." Certainly the young Glyn Simon spurned popularity and rejoiced in the role of the *enfant terrible*. He had no fear of controversy or of Press publicity ; indeed he seemed to court them. He was determined, impatient, and sometimes devious, in obtaining his ends ; he was often provocative in speech. Thus he gained the admiration of many, but he also aroused the suspicion of many more.

"Towards the end of my time, however, I became more acceptable in such quarters." With increasing responsibility came a greater readiness to listen and a greater patience in resolving conflicting opinions. Even the most suspicious could not but recognise that the more mature Glyn Simon stood resolutely for the historic Faith in times of change. He combined a radicalism which attracted the young with a conservatism that reassured the old, and both came to appreciate his qualities.

"Outside the Church I do not think I would have been heard in the rough struggle for survival in the surrounding jungle." These words indicate that the old wound from his schooldays did not heal completely ; and that he was always conscious of a basic lack of self-confidence which may not have been apparent to others but which must have added to the strain of public life.

"But in the Church and in its Ministry I found not only a challenge but an opportunity." The Church provided him with a platform which he used to good effect. That he responded to the challenge and seized the opportunity cannot be denied. He was described in an English periodical as "by common consent the diocesan one would most like to have".[27] Nearer to home, one who directed the many radio and television programmes in which Glyn Simon was involved writes : "What shone through on all the numerous broadcasts I did with him over a wide range of subjects was a positively luminous aura of true humility which always made a rare impact on the listeners or viewers. He commanded attention and respect and elevated himself, if that was possible, into an undenominational spokesman for the caring people in our society."[28]

"Such gifts as I have I was forced to use and did for good or ill." He was too much of an activist for his literary remains to be more than slight, a few small books, some articles, some printed sermons and speeches ; but he caught the attention of his listeners, individuals, groups, even consultants at the Lambeth Conference, by his clarity of thought and by his informed expression.[29] By his sympathetic awareness of the many facets of Welsh life he became truly "Archbishop of Wales" and a spokesman for the Principality. Despite his limitations in the use of the Welsh language he made a greater impact upon the Welsh consciousness than many who had started without his disadvantage.[30] He spoke to his generation as a prophet. By his keen and forthright analyses of the problems of the times of change his voice was heard far beyond the borders of his native land ; and the Province of Wales became known for the prophet that had arisen in its midst.

NOTES

Unacknowledged quotations are from letters and papers at the National Library of Wales which are not at present available to the general public.

1. Here & Above : MS Reminiscences of Glyn Simon.

2. Details above are owed to the Rev. K. Thompson, the late Canon Frederic Hood and Lord Wicklow.

3. Details above are owed to the Right Rev. E. S. Thomas, The Ven. T. Bayley Hughes, Canon T. J. Morris & Fr. Silyn Roberts.

4. Quoted in J. G. W. Farley, *Pull No More Poles*, 1962.

5. T. Worsley, *Flannelled Fool*, 1966, p. 47.

6. Here & above : letters in the possession of the Ven. C. Witton-Davies.

7. I owe this to the late Mr. George Pace who told me that the references to the proposed painting in M. Collis, *Stanley Spencer*, 1962, p. 233 ; and Sir John Rothenstein, *Time's Thievish Progress*, 1971, pp. 65-6, are incorrect.

8. *The Times*, 22 June, 1972.

9. Ms of Canon Edwin Davies.

10. Ed. E. W. Kemp, 1955 : see Zech. XI. 7.

11. *Bishops*, Ed. Bp. of Llandaff, 1961, p. 9.

12. *Arch. Cam.*, 1966, p. 4.

13. I owe this to the Rev. P. M. K. Morris.

14. Here & below : letters of the Ven. C. Witton-Davies.

15. *Towers and Spires*, 1908 : *Parish Church Architecture*, 1924 : *Baptismal Fonts*, 1928.

16. Liverpool, Guildford, Coventry and Bristol R. C. Cathedral.

17.   *Western Mail*, 21 Jan. 1960.

18.   *Ibid.* 2 April, 1960.

19.   "To my wife, most loving and most sweet, who awaits the glorious resurrection".

20.   I owe this section to the MS of the Rev. D. S. Lee.

21.   I am grateful to Mr. Gareth Bowen, Editor of 'Good Morning, Wales' and to the B.B.C. for permission to print the typescript of the programme.

22.   Letters above quoted with the permission of Mr. Edward Heath and Lord Greenwood.

23.   Abbreviations for British and World Councils of Churches, Missionary Councils, Moral Rearmament, the Missionary and Ecumenical Council of the Church Assembly, and the United Nations Works Relief Agency for Palestine and the Near East.

24.   David Walker : *A History of the Church in Wales*, 1976, p. 178.

25.   Glanmor Williams, "Diocese of St. Davids etc.". *Journal of the Historical Society of the Church in Wales*, Vol. XXV., 1976, pp. 25-6.

26.   I owe this to Dafydd Iwan.

27.   *Prism*, Feb. 1964, p. 11.

28.   Letter of Mr. Gareth Bowen.

29.   I owe this to Canon A. M. Allchin.

30.   In the opinion of the late Aneirin ap Talfan Davies.